Pendulum Mojo

How to Use Truth Testing for Clarity, Confidence, and Peace of Mind

Amy Scott Grant, MBA

Spiritual Ass Kicker

Castle Rock, CO

Published by Liberto Press
Castle Rock, Colorado, USA
© 2015 Amy Scott Grant
Book design, cover, and production by LibertoPress.com
Editing by Deb McLeod of DebMcLeod.com
Photographs and digital illustrations by Andrew E. Grant

Although the author and publisher have made every effort to ensure that the information in this book was correct at press time, the author and publisher do not assume and hereby disclaim any liability to any party for any loss, damage, or disruption caused by errors or omissions, whether such errors or omissions result from negligence, accident, or any other cause.

Some names and identifying details have been changed to protect the privacy of individuals.

This book is not intended as a substitute for the medical advice of physicians. The reader should regularly consult a physician in matters relating to his/her health and particularly with respect to any symptoms that may require diagnosis or medical attention. It is wise to drink plenty of water during (and immediately following) any kind of energy work.

Library of Congress Catalog Number: 2015900646
ISBN: 978-0-9862269-3-9
First Liberto Press printing, February 2015

DEDICATION

This book is dedicated to my
amazing daughter Sally,
who designs the most beautiful
pendulums I have ever seen.

Girl, you've got the Pendulum Mojo, fo sho.

TABLE OF CONTENTS

Why a Pendulum Book By a Spiritual Ass Kicker? 3

Lagniappe: My Gift to You 5

Chapter One: Welcome to the Pendulum............................ 7

Chapter Two: How to Use a Pendulum 19

Chapter Three: How to Ask......................................25

Chapter Four: Mojo and Special Uses....................................59

Chapter Five: Bias and Third Party Verification 93

Chapter Six: Pendulum Myths & Urban Legends..............99

Chapter Seven: Weird Other Stuff 105

Conclusion.. 114

Where to Buy a Pendulum....................................... 117

Get Your Mojo Back! 118

About the Author 121

WHY A PENDULUM BOOK
BY A SPIRITUAL ASS KICKER?

Greetings and salutations from Earth. Yep, that's where I live: on Earth. If you were expecting a Birkenstock-wearing, patchouli-smelling, hairy armpitted old soul named Moonbeam or Cosmic Sparkles, prepare to be disappointed. I'm a straight-talkin', sure-shootin', joke-crackin' intuitive healer with a strong connection to the Divine, an intense aversion to bullshit, and both feet planted firmly on the ground. (Okay fine, I'm an old soul, too.) That, dear Seeker, is the Spiritual Ass Kicker.

When I first learned to use a pendulum back in 2007, I immediately loved it. But I struggled to plod my way through any books available on the topic. To me, they were either too heady and bogged down in diagrams and analytics, or they were too airy-fairy and nonspecific. I was left with more questions than answers, and ultimately learned to trust my intuition and develop my own simplified systems and processes.

Since that time, I've taught hundreds of thousands of individuals how to use a pendulum for Truth Testing to make their lives better and easier. Even those who already knew how to use a pendulum for basic yes/no testing loved the new tips and techniques they picked up from me. You may have seen my YouTube videos on how to use a pendulum, or you may be here simply to learn more about dowsing.

No matter what brought you to this page, it is my goal that by the time you finish reading this book, you will have everything you need to master Truth Testing with a pendulum, and all your questions will be answered. That's Pendulum Mojo.

Besides a Spiritual Ass Kicker, I'm also a master intuitive healer, hilar-voyant (hilarious+clairvoyant), speaker, best-selling author, and badass thought leader. I have permanently cleared millions of blocks for thousands of people across more than thirty countries. I've created dozens of programs and premium courses and I get jaw-dropping results for teachers, accountants, sales people, entrepreneurs, moms, executives, coaches, artists, analysts, healers, and others just like you.

My full bio (plus a couple of sneak surprises) can be found in the *About the Author* section at the end of this book.

But enough about me, this book is all about **you** and what you can do with a little Pendulum Mojo. Let's dive in!

LAGNIAPPE

In my hometown of New Orleans, we use the word **lagniappe** (pronounced *lan-yapp)* to mean "a little something extra." Here's a little lagniappe for you.

Have you ever wished you could have an **Easy Button** for life? Now you can!

This powerful yet simple tool will assist you in making countless decisions and choices throughout your day, and you can rest easy knowing you're always making the most optimal decision on any matter in any given moment.

Plus, you can use this tool to discern whether someone is telling you the truth or not. How many situations can you think of where *that* would come in handy?

Visit **www.InfoYesNo.com** to claim your free Truth Testing mini-course, a $97 value and the perfect accompaniment to this book.

CHAPTER ONE:
WELCOME TO THE PENDULUM

What Is a Pendulum?

A pendulum simply refers to a long chain or string with a heavier object on one end, which is free to swing. Galileo is said to have been the first to discover the pendulum as a measure of time, but the exact origin of the pendulum as a tool for testing information, dowsing for water, etc., is unknown. It is safe to say pendulums have been used as spiritual tools for centuries.

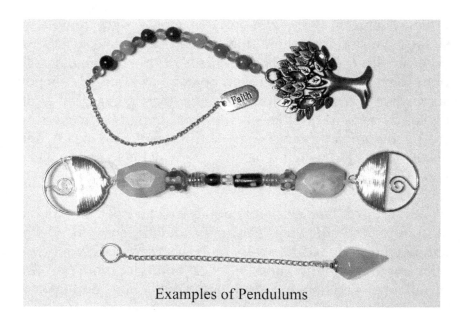

Examples of Pendulums

In the context of this book, I will show you how to use a pendulum for Truth Testing and healing work. I use the phrase "Truth Testing" to refer to any systematic process for verifying or ascertaining what is true. But as you will see, dear Seeker, the pendulum can do a whole lot more for you and can make your life simpler, more streamlined, happier, and more productive. Likewise, using a pendulum can build your confidence, your intuition, and your self-reliance. But we will get to that soon enough.

Where Can You Find a Pendulum?

You can make a pendulum from objects lying around your home, or you can buy one. Check your local area for a metaphysical shop, a spiritual bookstore, or a gemstone store (what I like to call a "rock shop").

Alternatively, you can fashion a makeshift pendulum from ordinary objects you have in your home right now. The simplest version is to slip a ring onto a chain or necklace, but you can also tie a washer onto a piece of string, slide a needle onto some thread, or pick up an object that is already shaped somewhat like a pendulum (a cell phone charger, a small digital camera, a set of keys). The main thing is to make sure the pendulum can swing freely, and that you can clearly and visibly be certain which direction it's swinging in at any given time.

If you want a fancier pendulum, you can special order a custom pendulum from **CustomPendulums.com.** If you're handy with some basic jewelry tools, you can make your own but as you and I both know, it'll cost you a lot more because of all the additional fun things you'll buy during that enthusiastic trip to Hobby Lobby or Michael's.

How to Pick the Right Pendulum

People often ask me how they can be sure they're picking the pendulum that's really right for them, and the answer is quite simple. Use a pendulum to check in. Oh wait, I forgot. You don't have a pendulum, right? I'm kidding. But seriously, if you're lucky enough to visit a store that has a selection of many great pendulum choices, you can just pay attention and notice which one wants to come home with you. For starters, does one seem to catch your eye or jump out at you? Try not to analyze why it happened (oh, I must have been drawn to that one because it's orange and my favorite time of day is sunset); just roll with it. Secondly, pick it up and notice how it feels in your hand.

The very first pendulum I bought was a small, simple, ordinary looking pendulum—the kind you find in any metaphysical shop around the globe. The pointed end was a lapis lazuli stone, midnight blue with gold flecks, and I loved it. I still have it, in fact. I knew from the instant I picked it up that it was mine and it would come home with me.

Of course, I didn't know jack about crystals then, so I got completely hosed on the price, but who cares? I'm a bit wiser with my money now, and besides, I just love that pendy so much. Weird fun fact: that pendulum always has, and continues to this day, to only answer questions of a spiritual nature. More about that later.

Lastly, before you choose a pendulum, take it for a test drive. See how it functions for you. I'll get into the particulars of that in the next chapter, but if you're really concerned about getting the right, perfect pendulum (because I know some people actually do worry about that) then fashion a temporary one for now, and when you finish this book it's time to go pendulum shopping.

Incidentally, I have about a dozen pendulums around my house at any given time. The kids have a few, I keep one next to my bed and one or two on my desk, my husband has several, and you will find pendulums here and there throughout my space. The lapis lazuli pendulum is always in my purse (just in case I'm out of the house and find myself with a sudden and pressing question of a spiritual nature, of course), and we sometimes have one in the car, too. What can I say? I like options. But I have also known individuals who own only one pendulum, and it is always on their person, hence they see no need to own more than one.

My point? Pendulums are as personal as underwear. There are plenty of types of underwear to choose from. There's cotton, nylon, spandex, lace, and even edible undies. There's high-rise, low-rise, string, boy shorts, thongs, boxers, briefs, long underwear, and granny panties. And they come in all colors and textures, too, and you probably have a variety in your underwear drawer right now, although some people may have all the same kind, all in white. Unless you don't wear underwear, you buy and you choose and you stock up according to your preference.

Same goes for pendulums. There are big ones and small ones and plain ones and fancy ones and long ones and short ones, and even a category I call **mandulums,** a non-frou-frou pendulum designed especially for men.

Or you might prefer to go au naturel, and decide not use a pendulum at all (in which case, I'm not sure why you bought this book).

Pendulums are personal. Go with what you like, don't sweat it if your preferences change over time, and don't let anyone else talk you into or out of a pendulum that resonates with you. In the same way a chef develops a personal relationship with his or her knife, you will develop a personal relationship with your pendy, so what say we make sure you start off on the right foot, hmm?

What Makes a Pendulum Work? Where Do the Answers Come from?

There is no power in the pendulum itself; this is important to remember. It is you who has the power, and **you** who has access to all of the information and answers that you seek. The pendulum is merely a tool (albeit a powerful and useful one) to help you discover those answers. Now you will begin to see why the personal relationship is so important.

Consider that there is a higher version of you, linked to the Universe and everything in it. This connectedness gives you access to all information—past, present, and future. Such a connection imparts its wisdom, its guidance, and its infinite being-ness. The pendulum is one tool that allows you to access the higher version of you, this Higher Self, the infinitely divine being that is You.

When you get into your car, you tell the car to start by putting the key into the ignition and turning that key. You do not need to know anything about internal combustion, horsepower, or what the heck a "hemi" is in order to take that car from point A to point B. Rather, you just need to know how to drive it. It's exactly the same with your pendulum.

This book will show you how to drive your pendulum; how to operate it for maximum effectiveness (mojo). The more you use your pendulum, the easier and more streamlined your life will become, just as it did when Henry Ford changed lives with his Model T. Although, luckily, the pendulum emits no noxious fumes and its use leaves no carbon footprint. Plus, it's highly unlikely that you would ever die from operating a pendulum, even if intoxicated.

Can a Pendulum Really Make a Difference?

You have no idea just how big a difference the pendulum can make, but soon you will. By the time you finish reading this book, you will no longer have to take anyone's word for anything (including mine). So you'd better hope to God that your adolescent or prepubescent kid doesn't get a hold of this book because then you might be in for a world of headaches. Teenage rebellion is one thing, but rebellion backed by the power of Infinite Truth, well, that's a force to be reckoned with.

Why Use a Pendulum?

As you are about to discover, the use of a pendulum will streamline your decision-making process and allow you to make the most optimal choice possible at any given time. Let's take a look at some of the best-known uses for pendulum testing.

Common Uses for Pendulums

My first encounter with the use of a pendulum was for what I now refer to as **Truth Testing.** An energy healer was working with me and she taught me to use a pendulum so that I could check in to validate that the clearing she had just performed on me was in fact complete. I liked this method immediately. I appreciated the self-reliance, the ability to check for myself, instead of just taking what she said at face value. It empowered me to know for myself that the healing had finished and was working. I soon found this method of verification to be useful in other avenues, such as decision-making.

There's nothing worse than being faced with a decision you feel ill-equipped to make. This causes a sense of being stuck, stymied, frustrated, or impotent. Personally, I value completion, certainty, and clarity, so discovering the pendulum as a way to check in and unequivocally know for sure the most optimal choice was a godsend to me. No more time wasted on the fence!

The pendulum helped me to make accurate, high-quality decisions and choices at lightning speed, and it can help you, too. It also helped me to know when it was not the right time to make that decision, and whether or not I needed to wait a day or two (or longer) to let the dust settle first.

Additionally, you can use a pendulum to help you determine whether or not a statement is true. This is useful in a variety of situations, from figuring out which one of your kids is telling the truth to checking the validity of something you read in a book (barring this one, of course, wink wink) or something a so-called expert tells you.

But besides these common uses for the pendulum, there are also a variety of additional methods, including but not limited to:

- ❖ Verifying allergies and sensitivities;
- ❖ Checking with your body to see what kind of effect a particular substance will create;
- ❖ Choosing what to eat in a restaurant;

❖ Booking your flight to ensure smooth travels with minimum hassle;

❖ Finding out whether a person is trustworthy or not;

❖ Transforming your relationship with money;

❖ Finding lost items (scrying);

❖ Setting prices for business or personal sale; assisting with price negotiations;

❖ Healing physical, emotional, and energetic blocks (one of my favorite pendulum uses, but this is a topic for a whole other book);

❖ Energetically clearing a room;

❖ And much more.

Advantages of Using a Pendulum

There are a number of advantages to using a pendulum for Truth Testing. Proper pendulum use provides reliable, unbiased answers, and a higher perspective than you could get on your own, especially in situations where you have a strong bias one way or another.

Additionally, the pendulum:

❖ Is small and unobtrusive.

❖ Is highly portable, and can be carried in a pocket or purse.

❖ May be plain and simple, elegant, or ornate and blingy.

- ❖ Is very easy to use.

- ❖ Can be adapted for a variety of uses.

- ❖ Is easy to teach others to use.

- ❖ Helps to strengthen your trust in the Universe and yourself.

- ❖ Builds your confidence.

- ❖ Gives objective answers.

- ❖ Confirms your intuitive hits.

- ❖ Can settle a bet, a sibling squabble, where to have dinner, and the "It wasn't me!" mystery.

- ❖ Lets you align with divine timing.

- ❖ Confirms or denies information that may appear suspect.

- ❖ Provides a second opinion in sensitive, legal, relationship, or medical matters.

- ❖ Assists you in making the best possible choices and decisions at any given time.

Caveats of Pendulum Use

As with anything, there are also some caveats to watch out for, although admittedly, the pendulum doesn't have many. For example:

- ❖ **It takes some time and practice to get good.** The upside is it's not as tedious as the violin, it doesn't take nearly as many hours to get good at, and while you're practicing, it won't sound like a wailing cat.

❖ **Your accuracy will increase with practice.** It's easy to get discouraged when you see some incorrect answers at first, but hang tight and keep at it. Generally, you want to work toward ninety-five percent (95%) accuracy, unless you're an overachiever like me, then you want ninety-nine to one hundred percent (99-100%). And you know who you are.

❖ **It might not move at all for you.** A very small percentage of people will see no movement at all with a pendulum. (Sorry, no refunds on this book, heh heh.) Usually this is caused by a prior lifetime as a witch or other sort of alternative healer where things did not end well for you. In most cases, a past life clearing is all it takes to resolve this and get some movement from the pendulum.

❖ **It requires patience at first.** If you're anything like me, you groan and roll your eyes anytime you see the word patience but the fact of the matter is, for most people, the pendulum takes awhile to start moving at first, which means every time you check in, it takes an extra couple of minutes. But with practice, you will get faster over time.

❖ **It can become addictive.** It's rare, but I have seen people become so obsessed with the pendulum that they cannot make a move without it. "All things considered, is it optimal for me to use the bathroom here, or wait until I get home?" It's a tool, not a substitute for your brain. As with everything, use in moderation. Except, a lot.

❖ **Some people may lose perspective.** It's important to remember that there is no power in the pendulum itself. It is your energy (the energy of your Highest Self) that gives the pendulum its power and ability. Using a pendulum is designed to help you become self-reliant on your inner guidance, as a way to verify those nudges and intuitive hits that you get on a day-to-day basis. It is not a replacement for common sense or inner guidance. Remember that, and all will be well in your world.

❖ **You could get carpal tunnel syndrome.** I've never actually heard of this happening from simply using a pendulum, but in the interest of full disclosure, I suppose it's possible. Here's a good rule of thumb: if you feel any discomfort while holding the pendulum, review the section in this book where I explain how to hold it properly, and adjust your position until you feel comfortable. Voilá. Crisis averted.

❖ **People might think you're weird.** Haven't you heard? Weird is the new normal. At least that's what I've been telling people. What, still concerned? Later in this book I'll show you an alternative way to Truth Test without pulling out an actual pendulum. Yes, Truth Testing can be discreet if you wish.

Now that we've looked at everything that could possibly go wrong (which, as you can see, is not much), let's get into the logistics of how to hold and calibrate a pendulum.

CHAPTER TWO:
HOW TO USE A PENDULUM

How to Hold a Pendulum

Once you become experienced with using a pendulum, you can hold it any old way you want but if you're a newbie, it helps to start out the way I describe here. This will assist you to get your bearings and avoid any mixed signals.

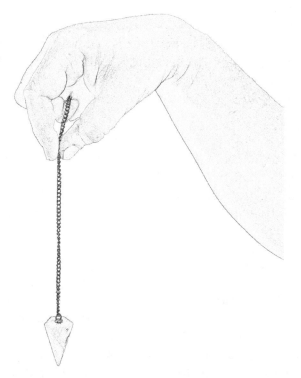

Figure 1. Recommended hand position for pendulum virgins and newbies.

Sit up with your back straight and your feet uncrossed and flat on the floor. Pick up your pendulum with your dominant hand and bend comfortably at the wrist. Imagine the energy is coming off your hand and down into the pendulum, like a waterfall.

Keep your elbow down to prevent your arm from getting tired. At first it can take a while until you get the hang of it and pick up speed. So for now, elbow down. It's best while you're first learning to avoid resting your elbow on anything.

The dangly part of the pendulum should be even with the middle of your chest, so that your pendulum hangs about six to eight inches in front of you, between your heart chakra and solar plexus. Relax your shoulder, your wrist, and your jaw. These are the places where most people hold tension, and tension is just a form of resistance, and resistance is what stops you from being able to do energy work. Relax your jaw and this will remind you to release tension elsewhere.

Remember, the pendulum can't do anything without a person, because the energy comes from the person, not the pendulum. If you have your shoulders scrunched up around your ears, how well do you think energy will flow through you? Relax. Breathe. Relax some more. Now you are ready to calibrate.

How to Calibrate

The word **calibrate** means to mark with a standard set of readings, and calibration with a pendulum is fairly simple. You will ask three separate questions with a pause between each to check the direction of movement, which will become your **sign** to represent that particular answer. It doesn't matter if your eyes are open or closed, but some people find it is easier to be patient when their eyes are closed as they wait for the pendulum to move. Here are the statements to say out loud or in your head:

Please show me a clear sign for **yes.**

Then wait for the pendulum to move and observe which way it's moving. If the direction is circular, notice whether it's clockwise or counter clockwise. Be patient and remain focused on the statement/question at hand, as it can sometimes take several minutes if this is your first time. Once you make a note of your sign for **yes,** go on to the next calibration statement.

Please show me a clear sign for **no.**

Again, wait for a clear and distinct movement, different from your sign for **yes.**

Please show me a clear sign for **need more info.**

This will be your third and final sign.

For now, all you need to know is whenever you ask a question and your pendulum shows you the sign for **need more info** it's best for you to revise the question and ask again.

Of note, if you receive a clear sign for **yes,** and then several minutes go by as you are waiting to see your signs for **no** or **need more info,** it is possible that one of those signs for you may be **no movement.** In other words, your **no** might be a perfectly still pendulum. Once you know your **yes,** you can verify this by asking, "Is **no movement** my sign for **no?**"

Next, I'll explain the most common signs for **yes**, **no**, and **need more info**, but your signs may be totally different, which is fine. Incidentally, your signs are like your car insurance; they travel with you, no matter what you're driving. If you get a new pendulum, or borrow a friend's, this will not cause your signs to switch.

Take a few minutes now to calibrate and discover your pendulum signs.

Universal Signs

There are some generally accepted (also called "Universal," as in the cosmos, not the theme park) signs, which are as follows:

Yes: Swings front to back, like a head nodding; or in a clockwise circle.

No: Swings side to side, like a head shaking no; or in a counterclockwise circle.

Need more information: Typically a diagonal swing (in either direction, although more commonly top left to bottom right); or no movement at all.

Do not be alarmed if you have signs that differ from these; it's more common than you may think. People often tell me about their strange alternate sign and ask me, "Is that normal?" Please. Are you telling me you're reading this book because you're really concerned with what's considered "normal"?

"Weird is the new normal."
~Amy Scott Grant

This is the weird, wacky, wonderful world of energy, love. It's all "normal." We calibrate so we know what your version of normal looks like. However, I will say that if you have alternative signs when you first learn to use a pendulum, you may want to calibrate often, as your signs may revert to the Universal signs at some point. But if some time passes and they're still out of the ordinary, then they're probably yours for good.

If at some point your signs convert to Universal signs, it is highly unlikely that they would change again after that, which means there's no need to calibrate further.

What to Think about While Asking

There are slightly different schools of thought when it comes to "what to think about" while you are waiting for your pendulum to reveal an answer. Some say you should keep your mind blank, while others recommend that you stay focused on the question. I know first-hand how hard it is to keep an active mind blank, so it's generally hard for me to do this with a pendulum. Therefore, I tend to recommend that you stay focused on the question at hand.

This serves three purposes: one, it's easier, which means you're more likely to do it (it's human nature to take the path of least resistance). Two, it keeps you from getting a false answer, which can happen if your mind wanders and you accidentally think of a new question, in which case your pendulum may answer the new question instead of the original question. Three, keeping your focus on the question itself (rather than the answer you'd prefer to see) reduces the risk of your bias influencing the pendulum's answer. Do what you want, but for me, I recommend staying focused on the question at hand.

Speaking of questions, let's move on and look at the proper way to phrase your question in order to ensure maximum accuracy.

CHAPTER THREE:
HOW TO ASK

The Formula for the Ask

The quality of the answer you get will be directly related to the quality of the question you ask. Therefore, it is essential to ask in as clear a manner as possible. The better you become at asking, the quicker your accuracy will improve, and the more satisfied you will be with your pendulum experience overall.

Begin your question with the phrase "all things considered." I recommend this wording because it covers all bases, not just what you want, or what your brain thinks, or what your emotions are pulling you toward in the moment. **All things considered** allows you to ask from a Divine perspective, across all time and space, transcending your mind and your conscious awareness. **All things considered** is all-encompassing, which means it produces a reliable answer based on a total 360-degree perspective (or perhaps 720 would be more accurate). It's like the difference between asking a question with a mere human brain and asking a question as an infinite being. Throughout this book, you will see it abbreviated as **"ATC."**

Next, it is best to avoid language that implies judgment. Consider that in Divine Mind it's all good. Therefore, you may not get reliable answers if your question contains judgmental words like "should," "can," "right/wrong," "good/bad," etc. More detail about that later in this chapter. For now, just know that it's best to stick with the highly effective yet neutral word, "optimal."

Many people find that when they begin to use a pendulum, they quickly develop an affinity for the word **optimal.** It's a delicious word, really, devoid of oppressive judgment or strict morality. Don't be surprised if this word weaves its way into your day-to-day language, or if someone in your life responds with, "Ooooh, **optimal.** I like that."

When you are mindfully creating your question, stick to whatever is within your scope of control right now. Truth Testing is ideal for making decisions and choices, and verifying whether something is true. "Is it optimal for me to call so-and-so?" is a far superior question to "Is so-and-so the right guy for me?" Likewise, "Is it optimal for me to submit my résumé to XYZ Company?" is much better than "Is XYZ Company going to hire me?" Focus on what you can do right now, and ask questions that lead you to discover the best choice or decision now, in this moment.

Lastly, since you are looking for a **yes/no** answer, stick to just one variable per question. If you could only answer **yes** or **no** and someone asked you if you would like five thousand dollars that can be found inside an elephant's ass, you would probably be stumped. Not just because you're wondering where this person has been hanging out lately (zookeeper gamblers anonymous?), but you could not answer if you wanted to say **yes** to five thousand dollars, but **no** to going head-first into an elephant's poop shoot. Whereas if you were asked, "Would you like five thousand dollars?" you could easily answer **yes** and then when asked if you'd like to fish it out of an elephant's rectum, you could (and hopefully, would) politely decline with **no.** Yes, you are now free to poke out your mind's eye.

One variable at a time makes it easier to get a **yes/no** answer from your pendulum. If you get a **need more info** sign, it is likely that you sneaked in more than one variable without meaning to do so.

Here are some examples of well-phrased Truth Testing questions:

All things considered, is it optimal for me to have lunch with Jessica?

ATC, is it optimal for me to book my flight to Jamaica?

ATC, is it optimal for me to hire Jackie for babysitting?

ATC, is this meat optimal to eat? Alternatively, you could ask: all things considered is this meat safe to eat without risk of food poisoning?

ATC, is Bertha (an employee) stealing office supplies?

Whereas, these are examples of poorly phrased questions:

Should I go out with Michael?

Notice the inherent judgment in the word "should." The Universe doesn't think you should or shouldn't do anything; that's why you have free will. Better to ask if it's optimal.

Is this the best job for me?

Again, we feel a sense of judgment around the word "best." Some people ask about their "highest and best" but the Universe would likely say, "What is the meaning of 'best'? Do what makes you happy."

Is Fluffy the poodle going to die?

There are a few issues with this question. First, it's clearly a prediction. We'll cover predictions in the "What Not to Ask" section. Second, yes, Fluffy will die. We all will, eventually, but that's cool because we'll be back. You think this is your first rodeo? Hardly.

The third and most important issue with this question is that it's not kosher to ask when a person will be born or when they will die. Again, focus on what's under your control.

If you're scheduling a c-section for your yet-to-be-born baby, then yes, you should check in and see what's the most optimal day to schedule that c-section. Otherwise, if it's to be a natural birth, be prepared and let the baby decide.

Is Santa Claus real?

Yes, Virginia, there is a Santa Claus. If you're too young to know what that means, please Google the previous sentence.

P.S., I recommend you have a couple of tissues handy when you do. (The fault in the question is that the truest answer is "It depends on what you believe.")

Is Beverly drunk?

This strikes me as an "It's none of your business" kind of question. Why do you need to know? Are you just being nosy, or are you wondering whether it's safe for her to drive home vs. call her a cab? If that's the case, a better question would be: "All things considered, is it optimal to call a cab for Beverly?"

What's my phone number?

Uncool question for the pendulum. Read ahead to the section called "Parlor Tricks" for a full explanation.

All things considered, does this pendulum make my butt look big?

Are you kidding? It's so slimming, you should buy two and wear 'em as earrings. Rrrrrrow!

Once you've calibrated and phrased your question properly, the last step is simply to relax and await movement, to discover your answer.

This is the simplest, yet sometimes the most challenging part of using a pendulum. When you first begin, it may take several minutes before you see movement. It will get faster with practice. Stay focused on the question until the pendulum begins to move.

Alternatively, you can distract yourself by clearly phrasing the question, then looking away for a bit. Think of Yoda perhaps. *Patience, young Jedi. Get answer you shall.* Then, when you see movement out of the corner of your eye, remove yourself from the Dagobah swamp and look to the pendulum for your answer.

Anyone can use a pendulum, even children. You can also test another person (or even an animal) by proxy, which can prove very useful in assessments, medical treatments, and healing work.

What Not to Ask

When I first learned to use a pendulum, I was told never to ask when someone will be born, or when they will die. I wasn't given a reason why I shouldn't ask these things, I was just instructed not to ask.

What I have found through experience is that you can ask anything you want, but as I mentioned earlier, keep in mind that **the quality of the answers you get will directly depend on the quality of the questions you ask.**

If you ask when a person will die, this is a prediction, which will probably not yield a reliable answer (more about that soon). Besides which, it helps to remember that individuals have free will, and they are also free to change their minds. I once knew a woman who was certain her mother had mere days remaining on earth. The woman was very old, and had already expressed that she felt complete and was ready to go any time. The family made life plans accordingly. Yet six months later, their mother was still going strong and showing no signs of an early departure. You just never know, and in some ways, it feels like none of your business to know. Treat everyone with the wonder and respect of the present, and let death take care of itself, in its own time.

Asking when a person will be born is also a prediction, which means you are unlikely to get reliable information. However, there are times when it is helpful to know the approximate time or date of a person's birth, simply for planning purposes. Here's how to handle that.

Let's say that your favorite niece is about to give birth to her first child, and you have promised to be there when she does. However, you live thousands of miles away, and perhaps you are concerned with the logistics of following through on this promise. For example, how much will a last-minute plane ticket cost? Will you be able to take spur-of-the-moment time off work? The first child usually comes after the due date, sometimes more than a week afterward, so you probably don't want to get there too early and wear out your welcome before the baby is born.

There would be several advantages to knowing the birth date in advance, in order to facilitate the planning of your trip. You know how a woman is when she's pregnant with her first child, right? It's all about the baby, and she just wants you there. With everything on her mind, plus the hormonal shifts, and overall discomfort of the third trimester, your niece isn't likely to be thinking about how difficult this could be for you, or frankly, how much it could cost you to disrupt your life to hop on a cross-country plane with just a day's notice.

But being present for the birth of a new member of the family is so special and precious, it would be worth it. And yet, since life wasn't mean to be a constant pain in the ass, consider that there is an easier way.

While it may not be useful to ask, "Will my niece's baby be born on her due date?" there are other questions that can be of great use to you in this planning process. Before you take a look at those possibilities, consider how effective it would be to first set an intention.

What is it that you want? Do you want to be present, at the hospital on the day the baby is born, so that you can support your niece and hold your newborn grandniece or grandnephew? Do you want to be in town to support her by cooking or helping with the baby during those first few days, or perhaps to care for her pets while she is in the hospital giving birth? What is it that you really want to happen for this event?

Once you know what you want, set a clear and precise intention, which might look something like this:

Example #1: I feel so blessed to be here with my niece and her new baby. I am happy to be able to help her transition into this new and wonderful phase of life.

Example #2: I am so grateful to be able to help my niece with her new baby, so that her partner can continue to work and support their family. It means a lot to be here for my niece when she needs me, and I'm overjoyed to be able to get to know this new little blessing.

Example #3: This has been the very best visit my niece and I have ever had! We talked and connected and shared the wonder and awe of this newborn baby. I'm so glad I was here to experience this and to deepen our bond.

Example #4: Wow. This trip confirmed two things for me: first, I love my niece more than anyone in the world and I'm so grateful she is in my life. Secondly, I made the right choice not to have children because they are wonderful but require a shocking amount of time and attention, which is definitely not right for me. I am so grateful for my freedom, and I have finally released my concerns about "what if?" Now I can head home for some peace and quiet and I'll visit again in a few months once the baby is sleeping through the night.

These are just a few examples. Sure, the fourth one is a bit tongue-in-cheek, but I put it in because I think it's important to realize that not all intentions are love and light and rainbows. Sometimes we set intentions about letting go, and there is a sense of "Thank goodness that's gone!" about it. Welcome to spirituality in the real world.

Now that you've set your intention, the next step is to begin asking questions about the factors that you can control. In this example:

❖ Whether or not to book your flight, or fly last-minute;

❖ When to book your flight, and whether or not to keep it open-ended;

❖ Whether to stay with your niece, with other relatives, or to book a hotel (I recommend first discussing it with your niece and her partner, of course);

❖ Decisions related to your work, such as whether to take time off or work while you're traveling; whether or not to book clients in the days surrounding the due date;

❖ Whether or not this is the right time to make these travel decisions;

❖ How to fund the trip: whether or not to budget money, or to take on an extra client or work overtime to pay for it, etc.;

❖ Whether or not it's optimal for you to arrive before the baby is born or after, depending on the intention you've set and what you want to accomplish;

❖ Whether or not to use reward miles to pay for your trip;

❖ Whether or not to find business to incorporate into the trip, if there is a possibility of creating the trip as a tax write-off;

❖ And anything else relevant to choices and decisions regarding this particular trip.

When we look at it this way, it's remarkable how many facets of this situation are actually within your control. Isn't that empowering? I love shifting my perspective from "Oh crap, how is this going to work without me getting screwed?" to "I have decisions to make about what kind of experience I'd like to create here." This is a sure way to shift from trapped and confused into clear and powerful.

Here are some of the questions you might ask in order to make the most optimal choices for your trip. I have abbreviated **all things considered** as **ATC.**

❖ ATC, is it optimal for me to be in (city of expected baby's birth) in time for the birth?

❖ ATC, is it optimal for me to make travel plans now? **(NOTE:** If you get no, you can skip the rest of this list and just check back in a day or three.)

❖ ATC, is it optimal for me to fly or drive?

❖ ATC, is it optimal for me to take off work for this visit?

❖ ATC, is it optimal for me to discuss my plans with my niece now, before I make any decisions?

❖ Etc. Based on the list above (what you can control) I think you get the idea.

Remember, the quality of the answers you get will directly depend on the quality of the questions you ask.

Think about what you really want to know (and why you want to know it). Consider what is within your scope of control right now, and then formulate the questions that will help you make the best possible choices.

Oh and as a side note—when you check in to ask when anything will happen, you might consider that the Universe has a funny way of looking at time. "Soon" could mean ten years from now, and if you consider the billions of years of existence so far, it kind of makes sense. In other words, don't get pissed off if you ask how long and the answer is "soon" and you feel as though you're growing old waiting for "soon" to play out. Live your life where it's meant to unfold: in the present. **Stay focused on using your pendulum and ask about choices you can make right now and you can't go wrong.** (If you really want to know *why* predictions aren't good Truth Testing questions, keep reading through to the "No Predictions" section.)

Parlor Tricks

Sometimes when I show someone how to use a pendulum, the first thing they want to do is a trick. This makes me sigh and drop my head. Really? I've just given you a key to unlock the wisdom of the ages and to make your life easier and more amazing than ever, and you want to use a pendulum to guess your best friend's childhood phone number? Jeez, a little perspective, please.

But the worst part is that then the person gets all up in a huff because "Hey, it didn't work!" How can they ever trust their pendy now, when it couldn't even recite a simple phone number?

This is not a parlor trick, people. We are not Sideshow Bob, hawking passers-by to "Come and witness the amazing powers of the ancient pendulum! Only twenty dollars a person!" We are spiritual beings having a human experience and your soul is literally thousands of years old, so can we please show a little maturity here?

The best way to learn to trust your pendulum is not to ask it questions that you already know the answer to (Is my name Amy? Do I have black hair? Is my hair amazing?), or questions you don't really want to know the answer to (What was the name of the kid who grew up in the house behind mine? What is the capitol of Kersplakistan? What size bra did Aunt Judith wear before she died?) This sort of "prove-it-to-me" thinking backfires in nearly every case.

To some degree, I understand the desire to want proof in a quick and easy manner. After all, we've all had the experience of getting scammed at one point or another, or making a bad decision based on someone else's advice. As a newbie, you don't want to use your pendulum for guidance on a major decision, and then later find out you misread the signs or didn't phrase the question properly. Nobody wants to get hosed like that. But there are better ways to get proof.

What if you were to treat this spiritual tool with dignity and respect? Open your heart to the experience and see what happens.

If you want proof, go about it in this way:

For the next twenty-four hours, use your pendulum to make

small choices throughout your day. Examples:

- ❖ ATC, is it optimal to take the stairs or the elevator?
- ❖ ATC, is it optimal to bring my lunch or eat lunch out today?
- ❖ ATC, is it optimal to wear these shoes?
- ❖ ATC, is it optimal to watch this television show?

Next, observe what happens. Write down your observations. Notice when anything unusual or synchronistic happens.

This is where your proof can be found. This is irrefutable proof, too. Because otherwise, if you ask the pendulum to reveal your family's telephone number when you were an infant, even if it does, and gets it right, some part of you will dismiss the validity, saying "Oh, it was probably lodged in my subconscious memory somewhere." You won't really believe in the guidance provided by the pendulum.

But if you have choices where you don't care one way or the other (bring lunch or buy lunch, for example), and you check in with your pendy, and then something amazing happens as a result, then you can see first-hand the irrefutable benefits of Truth Testing.

If you think these small, seemingly insignificant choices don't matter in life, you are gravely mistaken.

I went through a period of time where I let my jewelry choose itself. Sometimes I used the pendulum; other times, I simply opened my jewelry box and asked, "What wants to be worn today?" But I allowed myself to be guided in my jewelry choices. Shortly afterwards, I met someone who quickly became one of my closest friends. We met because I was wearing a particular ring, a ring with a stone called Larimar, which is nearly always mistaken for turquoise by the untrained eye. This is how the "chance encounter" went:

"Oh, I see you're wearing a Larimar ring."

"Yes, I am."

"They say Larimar is the lost stone of Atlantis," she said with a mysterious smile.

Instantly, I liked her, and a great friendship was born. But what makes this incident so interesting is that just days before I met Jen (that's her name, did I mention that?), I had set the intention to meet more people in my local town who were into spiritual stuff like me. Plus, as she and I were talking, we discovered that she had actually seen my pendulum videos on YouTube. Consider that my work is done entirely remotely and globally—I have no clients or students in my own town, intentionally. All of my marketing is done online, and at the time that I met her, only about 50,000 people in the world had seen those videos, and here I was now talking to one of them, who lived less than five miles from my house and had kids around the same ages as mine.

Would Jen and I have met if I hadn't worn that Larimar ring on that particular day? I can't say for sure, but I know the ring is the thing that instantly sparked a conversation with more depth than, "So, where do your kids go to school?" I also know I'm glad as hell I listened when that ring spoke up on that morning and said, "Me, me! Wear me today!"

These are the kinds of mini miracles that happen when you use Truth Testing. Start small. Use your pendy to make small choices throughout your day, and then see what kind of magic unfolds. Let this be your proof. And Google anything you want to know about Aunt Judith or addresses and phone numbers. (Stalker.)

No Predictions

At least twice already you've heard me say you can ask anything you want with a pendulum, but stay away from predictions because you won't get reliable answers, right? This is the one part of Truth Testing that people tend to get hung up on. Since I've advised you against making predictions, I'll now explain why.

By the way, I totally understand why we sometimes want the predictions. We want to know if we'll land the job or marry the guy or win the award or score the opportunity. We want to know if Grandma will pull through, if that blood test will come back negative, or if tomorrow will be a better day. I get it, I really do.

Have you heard of Chaos Theory? If you've seen or read Michael Crichton's *Jurassic Park,* you've at least heard of it. (By the way, how sexy is Jeff Goldblum in that film? Ai-yi-yi.) The **butterfly effect** is a chaos principle, which says that one tiny change in a nonlinear system can bring drastic changes down the road. If you've ever watched any movie that includes time travel, you know what I'm talking about.

Would I have met my friend Jen if I hadn't worn that Larimar ring on that particular day? How would my life be different if I hadn't befriended Jen? I know one thing for sure: my home wouldn't be decorated nearly as nicely as it is now, since Jen helps me shop for home décor... a LOT.

Every day is a series of choices: what to eat, what to wear, what to say, what to do, where to go, and when. Every tiny choice that you make is affecting outcomes in your life. In other words, the universe is always in flux, forever moving and shifting and morphing. How many choices do you figure you make in a day? Researchers at Cornell University found that a person makes an average of 220 choices **about food** (just food!) every day. Your world is ever changing, largely due to the choices you make as you go about your routine.

All outcomes are subject to change, which means any prediction that is true right now, may not be true thirty seconds from now.

This is why I say you can ask anything you want, but the predictions will not yield reliable answers.

You might be thinking, "But isn't what to eat or wear or when to book a flight a prediction?"

Excellent question. I'll explain this nuance as best I can.

The questions that produce the most reliable answers are the ones that focus on the here and now; what's true or most optimal in this moment. Therefore, when you're standing in your closet, facing your clothing, and you ask, "All things considered, is it optimal to wear this blue dress today?" you are not making a prediction, because you are actually requesting guidance for a choice that must be made right here, right now.

A little later in this book, I'll show you how I always wind up on the best possible flight, sitting next to the best possible person, by using my pendulum to check in before I book the flight. Some people have a hard time understanding how this kind of checking in *isn't* a prediction. But if you consider the choices to be made in the here and now, you will see why it's a valid approach.

I may begin by asking whether this is the most optimal day or time to make the choice, and then by inquiring about the choice itself. I won't go into the specifics of booking a flight here, because I'll cover that in explicit detail in the section called "Traveling Assistance." For now, just stick to what's within your scope of control in this moment.

The same is true for deciding what to eat. If a friend texts me and asks if I want to go to lunch tomorrow, and I check in and ask, "All things considered, is it optimal to go to lunch with so-and-so tomorrow?" that's not a prediction, because I'm making the choice and the commitment right now. If my pendulum refuses to move and won't give me an answer, that's a good indication that this isn't the optimal time to make that choice. Perhaps something will happen later today (one of the kids comes home sick from school and needs to stay home tomorrow; or maybe a client will book into a midday time slot tomorrow before I have a chance to close the schedule; or perhaps the appointment on my calendar for noon tomorrow will suddenly get rescheduled) which would influence my decision. As a personal preference, I would prefer to wait and give the person a definite answer, rather than give my friend a quick response and then have to call and change my answer later.

Likewise, if I said **yes** and the friend asked me "What would you like to eat?" I don't have to predict what I'd like to eat tomorrow, I could wait and see what I feel like when the time comes to meet. But if this is the optimal time to make that decision, then I could use Truth Testing to check in and see which restaurant or type of cuisine is optimal. Capisce?

Here are some examples of predictive questions transformed into more suitable questions. For these examples, I used derivatives of questions people ask me a lot.

Will we get back together? ➔ ATC, is it optimal for me to release him/her?

You would be amazed at how often people ask me this question. Sometimes I have a definitive answer for them, like when I can see that they are not a good long-term match or when I can feel a sacred contract between them that will make it impossible to stay apart (regardless of whether or not they should). But really, this question expresses feelings of need, loss, and uncertainty. The people who ask this question are generally not in a good space when they ask it, and I can empathize. Uncertainty sucks.

This is why I generally recommend they shift the question to "Is it optimal to release this person?" because that brings them back to what they can control, right now. One caveat: just because it's not optimal to release the person doesn't mean they will get back together. Similarly, if the answer is **yes, release the person,** it doesn't mean they are split up for good. But at least the answer to the transformed question gives some closure and direction as to what's next, as opposed to the "Will we get back together?" question, which just raises more questions, no matter what the answer.

Is (name) the right guy/girl for me? Is (name) my soul mate? ➔ ATC, is it optimal for me to continue dating (name)?

This is another very popular question, which comes from people of all ages. Is this one "the one"? In my experience, there is no "one" for you, unless you happen to have a twinning energy with another person (in which case, you'd already know who was "the one"), but twinning is a topic for another book. Basic quantum mechanics shows us that in any given moment, there exists a wave of infinite simultaneous possibilities, and when you (as the observer) choose one option, the entire wave collapses into that one possibility. Yes, I'm simplifying a very complex theory, but this is how our amazing world works. String theory exists well outside the parameters of the set of "The Big Bang Theory."

Is there only one soul mate or right person for you? Well, that would be one option that exists within the wave of possibilities. But if you haven't met that person yet, it does seem to put an inordinate amount of pressure on you and the potential relationship, doesn't it? You might choose instead to believe that there is a wave of possible soul mates for you. Which resonates more strongly with you? Which feels more expansive, more empowering?

I recommend focusing on what you can control, here and now, which is whether or not to continue dating this person. Again, just because the answer is **yes,** that doesn't mean the person is your soul mate. You could check again in a month and the answer may be **no.** Then, if the person asks you to marry them, you could check in at that point to see what is optimal.

Like I always say, let's not worry until there's something to worry about. Keep your focus in the present and all will be well in your world.

Are they going to offer me this job? → ATC, is it optimal for me to apply elsewhere?

It's nerve-wracking to wait to hear from a potential employer, especially if you're currently out of work. Worst of all, some employers don't have the decency to inform you if you didn't get the job. Sitting and waiting is the pits, and pretty soon, you start to wonder if you should call or email and follow up. What if they're waiting to hear from you, to see if you show initiative, or how much you want the job? Or what if they've hired another candidate and neglected to follow up with you? Or what if they're waiting on someone else (the higher-ups, the HR department, etc.) and your follow-up is viewed with disdain as a sign of impatience or desperation?

Again, the solution (at least as far as Truth Testing goes) is to focus on what you can control, here and now. *Is it optimal to make some follow up calls to other places where you've applied? ATC, is it optimal to submit my résumé elsewhere? Is it optimal to look online to see what else may have opened up in my field?*

If you were my client, I'd advise you to create a distraction (or three) for yourself. Attack that list of irritations around your house. Catch up on your correspondence. Organize your closets and clean out the garage. Be productive while you wait. This helps to take your mind off the waiting and helps you release attachment to a specific outcome.

Will my business be successful? ➜ Am I currently on track to achieve (name the target)?

People tend to ask me this at the start of a new year, or a new project, or a new partnership, or a new business. The trouble is, "Will I be successful?" is a loaded question. Not only is it a prediction, but also it's also vague. What is meant by "successful"? If you eked out a miniscule profit, that would technically be considered successful, but it would likely fall short of your goals and expectations, right? Most people will not get a clear answer when they ask "Will my business be successful?" (which is usually why they come to me for clarification).

A better approach would be to create a specific target. This may be an income goal, a quantity of units sold, a specific type of recognition or achievement (President's Club, Million Dollar Club, for example), or some measure of growth. Once you've selected your primary target, you can ask if you are currently on track to achieve this target. For example, a real estate agent who has set all of her marketing for the year and is out hustling every day, can ask "All things considered, am I currently on track to achieve Million Dollar Sales status?" and if she gets **yes,** then she can keep plugging away, but if she gets **no,** then there's some digging to do to find out what more she can do. She would want to check in periodically (Quarterly? Monthly? Weekly? Depends on the business and the person) to ensure she stays on track.

Alternatively, you could ask, "Is there anything more that's optimal for me to do in order to achieve (target)?" If you get **no,** keep doing what you're doing, but if you get **yes,** you'll need to start digging to find out what more is required.

Am I pregnant/will I get pregnant/is it a boy or a girl?

Jeez, I dislike these. But when I first meet someone, if they discover I'm psychic, these are the types of questions they ask me. There are a few problems with these questions.

For starters, if a woman wants to know if she's pregnant, then she's clearly very early on in the pregnancy. Which means a lot could change… or go wrong. Therefore, I don't like to answer this question for strangers (although I will for friends or clients, but first I express the caveat above).

The "Will I get pregnant?" question is a straight-up prediction. If a person has been trying to get pregnant and it seems to be taking a long time, then we can check in and see "All things considered, is there a physiological block to my ability to conceive a child?" We can ask similar questions to see if it's an issue with the woman or the man, or an emotional issue, or some other kind of block. I have helped a number of my clients and friends conceive by using energetic tools and processes to enhance the actions—ahem—they're already taking.

You might think the "Is it a boy?" or "Is it a girl?" questions are pretty straightforward, but here's the rub. The sex organs begin to develop around nine weeks of gestation, and an ultrasound will reveal the baby's gender between sixteen and twenty weeks. Modern science says that the baby's gender is determined at *conception,* since the mother and father each pass on 23 chromosomes, and the newly fertilized egg has among these either two X chromosomes (female) or one X and one Y chromosome (male).

However, when you consider the wave of infinite possibilities, you might consider that the baby hasn't always made up its mind until the definitive ultrasound that reveals the genitalia. Add to that the fact that some males carry more feminine energy than others, and some females carry more masculine energy than average, and this further adds to the murkiness.

The bottom line is this: I wouldn't go stock up on pink or blue clothing and crib bedding just because the pendulum told you you're having a boy or a girl. Sometimes, the gender is clear from the start (as with my first and my third children), and third-party verification will unanimously confirm this. Other times, the information received is mixed (as it was with my middle child) and the only way to know for certain is with a clear ultrasound image. Incidentally, when this happens, it doesn't mean anything at all. We got all sorts of information before my middle daughter was born: it's a girl, it's a boy, it's twins, it's one boy and one girl, etc. Ultrasound confirmed **girl** and she is the girliest girl in our entire family. Go figure.

Even though the gender is supposedly determined at conception (according to modern science), consider that "Is it a boy or a girl?" is also a form of prediction.

You might notice I didn't include a transformed question above, and that's because **it depends.** If you think you might be pregnant, then check in before you eat (ATC, is it optimal for me to have sushi today? ATC, is it optimal for me to have a glass of wine?). Better yet, stop at the drugstore and pick up a pregnancy test. If you are pregnant, but you're still waiting for your 20-week ultrasound and you've just found the most adorable pink ruffled onesie that's on sale and you just can't pass it up, then check in and ask "ATC, is it optimal for me to buy this now?" Again, don't get too worked up if the answer is **yes.** You might actually be getting it for your sister who's having a girl, but doesn't even know she's pregnant yet.

Stick to what you can control, here and now.

Will (he/she/I) be all right? (Usually asked with regards to medical results or a specific diagnosis.)

It's torture to wait for results of a medical test or procedure, isn't it? Oh, I know, it's just the worst. But any way you slice it, asking about the results is a prediction. Look at the situation and ask instead: what is within my control? If you're thinking ahead to the possible diagnosis, perhaps you would feel better if you researched alternative treatments or nutritional therapy. If you just can't bear to think about what you'll do if the test comes back positive, yet there's nothing you can do about it right now but wait, then stop asking questions and create a distraction for yourself. Make it a happy one or a productive one, but go get busy. This is the best way to pass the time until you know for certain.

Hopefully by now, it's crystal clear why predictions aren't valid, and how to change predictive questions into valid ones. Next we'll look at variables and other issues to avoid.

Multiple Variables and General Shenanigans

Often, if you ask a question and get **need more info** as the answer, it simply means you need to rephrase the question. In most cases, there are multiple variables present, and that's what's throwing a wrench in the works. Here are a few examples of questions with single variables and multiple variables, so that you can begin to recognize the difference.

Single variable questions:

❖ ATC, is it optimal to order waffles?

❖ ATC, is it optimal to get the car washed?

❖ ATC, is it optimal to go to the park today?

❖ ATC, is it optimal to buy this book?

Multiple variable questions:

❖ ATC, is it optimal for me to get strawberry waffles with Mike at Clancy's? (four variables: strawberry, waffles, Mike, Clancy's)

❖ ATC, is it optimal for me to get the car washed today, after I drop off Mickey and before I go to the party? (three variables)

❖ ATC, is it optimal to walk to the park, rent a bike, and get some exercise? (three to four variables, depending on how you look at it)

❖ ATC, is it optimal for me to order this book on my Amazon Prime, using the money I earned from selling my vintage Princess Leia action figure, and pay the extra for one-day shipping? (crapload of variables)

Remember, with what we've learned so far, your pendulum can only definitively answer **yes** or **no.** Imagine a friend asked you, "Hey, do you want to grab lunch today at that new Yemenese restaurant? I hear their yak is to die for." It's easy enough for you to respond with, "I'd love to grab lunch, but I just had yak yesterday, so I'm pretty yakked out. How about we get some Tex-Mex instead?"

You answered **yes** to part of the question ("Do you want to grab lunch today?") but said **no** to another part of the question ("at that new Yemenese restaurant"). But that's not an option for your pendulum. If the most optimal choice for one variable is **yes,** but another is **no,** and you've crammed them into the same sentence, then your pendulum will have no choice but to answer "huh?" (need more info).

Likewise, sometimes you ask what appears to be an innocent question, with two variables that should be able to go hand-in-hand, and yet your trusty pendy still gives you the **need more info** brushoff. In these cases, it's likely that your *timing* isn't quite right.

For example, if you asked, "ATC, is it optimal for me to book my flight to Katmandu today?" you might get a **need more info** if it is in fact optimal for you to go to Katmandu, and it's optimal for you to fly there (thankfully, as a long plane trip certainly beats a slow boat to China followed by a grueling yak-back ride), but the **needs more info** would come into play if **today** is not the optimal day to book that flight.

Incidentally, divine timing is where recovering control freaks such as myself tend to get tripped up. We get nervous as we see the fares creeping upward, we get antsy about not having our plans nailed down yet, and we want to have it all completed so urgently that we may even go so far as to influence the answers just to get the damn flight booked already. But great rewards await those who can chillax a bit and wait for the right time to take that action, whether it's booking a transatlantic flight or following up with that potential client or making some other key decision.

In my experience, when I listen to the guidance I receive, I am blessed many times over, and major hassles are avoided. This is very reassuring to me, and helps me remember to relax the next time my "right now" tendencies flare up around a key action or decision. Likewise, when I go against divine guidance and do what I want to do for the sake of being right or for instant gratification, ninety-nine percent of the time it comes back to bite me in the ass. Which also serves to remind me to listen (dammit!) to the guidance I get in the future.

Stick to one variable per question and relax while you ask and you can expect to yield highly reliable answers.

Words to Avoid

As we discussed, you can use your pendulum to ask most

anything you want. But experience will show you that certain words and phrases are less effective than others. This reminds me of when I was a kid and I asked my parents, "can I...?" to which they retorted, "I don't know, *can* ya?" I would then have to rephrase the question to say, "may I please...?" and then they would respond. Usually with a **no,** which frankly kind of pissed me off. Which is probably why I've lived most of my life under the guidance of "I'd rather ask forgiveness later than have to ask permission now." Ha! In your face, Mom and Dad!

Here are some words and phrases to avoid when asking Truth Testing questions. Unlike Mom and Dad, I'll include some rationale, so that you can understand why these are not as effective as their counterparts. Hmm. Maybe I've still got some parental stuff to clear. I'll work on that now, as you read this:

Should. You may have heard it said that if you focus on what you should and shouldn't do then before you know it, you're "shoulding" all over yourself. (If that didn't make you smile, say that last sentence out loud, it's funnier that way.)

Consider that from the perspective of the Universe, there is no **should.** You have free will, kemosabe, which means the ball is perpetually in your court. Should you take a swing and return the volley? Only if you want to. Should you pull a McEnroe and pitch your racket and stomp off the court? Sure, if that's what floats your boat. It's a free Universe and you're the one calling the shots. When you elevate your perspective to the highest possible viewpoint, there are no **shoulds,** there is only how you want to play the game. Presumably, we are using the pendulum to get some guidance on the most optimal course of action, so instead of asking "should," how about asking, "Is it optimal to..."

Can/Could. These words are not effective for the same reasons as "should." Can't you just imagine the Universe saying, "I don't know, *can* you?" Actually, I have found the Universe to be very comical, so if I used my pendulum to ask a question like, "Can I...?" the Universe would probably crack up laughing and make a comment like, "Well, what do you think, Miss Infinite Being Who Is A Part of Me And I of Her? Can we do that, or do you think something is actually impossible for us?" If you were to use "may" instead of "can" or "could," I think you would get a similar answer. Your Highest Self would remind you that you can do anything you wish, and that you have the freedom, power, and permission to do so. Again, instead of "can/could/may," it would be better to ask, "Is it optimal to...?"

Right/Wrong. These often come up with Truth Testing newbies, especially those who have some underlying issues or beliefs about getting it right, fear of making a mistake or looking foolish, or some other form of perfectionism. Questions such as "All things considered, is this the right job/spouse/dwelling for me?" will not yield as accurate answers as those that include the preferred word **optimal.**

I have often said if the Universe wore a t-shirt, it would say, "It's all good." From the highest possible perspective, it is all good. This tends to ruffle the feathers of those who are entrenched in lower energies and more pain-focused mentalities. How could rape and murder and genocide be "all good?" and perhaps that is a topic for a different book, but it is the truth, and you can check me on that. (As long you as you ask, "ATC, is that statement true and accurate?" and not, "Is Amy *right* about that?")

Good/Bad/Best. These are judgment words, so they tend to yield inferior results when used in a Truth Testing question.

For example: "Is oatmeal good for my body?" or "Is oatmeal bad for my body?" would be better phrased as "All things considered, is it optimal for me to eat oatmeal?" An even better way to check this would be with the multiple-choice options I'll explain in the next chapter.

"Best" is a word that most of use a lot in our day to day language ("Have you tried the yak at that new Yemenese restaurant? It's the best!") and rightfully so. Who wouldn't want the best of something? We love superlatives most of all (get it?) and pepper them everywhere (haha) in our language. But when it comes to Truth Testing, consider that if the Universe believes "It's all good" then how can there be a best? Really put yourself in the shoes (so to speak) of the Universe for a moment. Now imagine you, as the Universe, were invited to dinner, where you were served lobster with drawn butter, Alpo dog food, salad lyonnaise (my personal favorite), braised yak, and Easy Cheese squirted fresh from its pressurized can, all on the same plate. As you tasted each, what would you think?

The Universe, in its infinite wisdom, would rave over everything. "OMS, have you tried the yak dipped into the easy cheese? It's magnificent! And this lobster is just divine with the Alpo. Seriously, you gotta try this!" Yep, it's all good. So you don't want to be asking "What's the best?" of someone who thinks Alpo is tasty, do you? Nope. Again, instead of "Is this the best?" stick with "Is this the most optimal?" and you can't go wrong.

NOTE: When the Universe is talking to me, it says "OMS" instead of OMG. As in, "Oh my self!" Yep, told you it was funny.

Will. I recommend avoiding the word "will" (unless that's your man's name, of course. Proper noun Will is always welcome.) because it predicates a prediction, and we've already covered why predictions make poopy questions in Truth Testing. **Will** would also include predictive phrases like "is going to." Stick to what you can control in this moment. If you want to know if that guy or girl is going to ask you out, you're better off asking if it's optimal to buy a new outfit or keep your evenings open this weekend or line up a tentative babysitter for Saturday night.

Judgment words. It's best to omit from your question any word that inherently includes a judgment, and replace it with **optimal.** For example, **nice, okay, better, enough,** etc.

I love the word **optimal** because it is a completely neutral word with no inherent judgment. When you bundle **all things considered** with the word **optimal** in your question, you've got a winning combination, because you are sprechen the same lingo as your Highest Self. Of course, you can check me on this:

*All things considered, is **optimal** the most optimal word to use when truth testing?*

What to Do with "Need More Info"

When you ask a well-phrased question and you receive an answer of **need more info,** it's usually an indication that you need to rephrase the question. Here's a quick checklist for handling the **need more info** answer:

1. **Review your question.** Did you include more than one variable? This is the most likely reason for a **need more info** result. Is the question vague? If you ask a vague question, you can expect to get what I call a "magic

eight-ball answer" like **need more info.** Reword your question clearly, making sure to include just one variable, and this will likely resolve into a **yes/no** answer.

2. If your question is clear and already has just one variable, ask the following: "**Is this the most optimal time to ask this?**" This will help you determine whether it's a timing issue. Sometimes the answer has not yet been determined (things are still in flux) and so it may not be optimal for you to inquire about this right now, until some dust settles and things fall more into place. Other times, something else (better/more optimal/more along the lines of what you really want) is on its way, so it's not time to make the decision yet. When you rush a decision that's not yet reached its prime time, you'll make a choice you're likely to regret. Relax into the divine timing of things and all will unfold perfectly.

3. If you get **yes,** this is the optimal time, then ask: "**All things considered, is it optimal for me to know this?**" (or "to have this information"). This will show you whether it's a **none of your business** question, and most often, this happens when you check in around other people. Remember, you can't mess with free will, which means if someone wants to keep their business private, they have the right to do that, in which case you will have trouble obtaining such information. So mind your own beeswax.

There are other reasons why you might get a **need more info** or alternatively, when your pendulum stands still and refuses to move. Some questions may be none of your business in that it simply isn't optimal to know. If your spouse is acting weird, you may start asking a bunch of questions and not getting anywhere with your pendulum, but what if it's because he or she is planning a special surprise for you?

4. If you get **yes** to both of the questions above (this is the optimal time, and it is optimal to know this) then **try changing the phrasing of your question, even if it essentially means the same thing.** For example, "All things considered, is it optimal to go to the gym today?" could be changed to "All things considered, is it optimal to work out today?" Even if you always visit the gym to work out, that simple word change-up could reveal that today it's optimal to go for a jog, or pull out one of your vintage Jane Fonda workout DVDs, or some other form of non-gym exercise.

5. **If all else fails, consult a thesaurus.** Sometimes (and this is rare) the meaning of a single word can trip you up. For example, I once had a conversation during which I got it was optimal for her to work with me for one-on-one coaching. I asked, "All things considered, is it optimal for me to coach Debra?" I got **yes** but Debra got **no.** This puzzled me, as my **yes** was clear, and I had no attachment or bias. In checking, I realized it was the word "coach" that was tripping her up. I changed the question to say, "All things considered, is it optimal for me to mentor Debra?" and without telling her the question out loud, I held the new question in my mind and asked Debra to check. She immediately got a clear **yes,** and when I explained what I had just done, Debra said, "That makes a lot of sense. I didn't have good experiences with coaches when I played sports, and I recently set the intention that I wanted to find a mentor for spiritual stuff and energy work." This

one-word trip-up is not common, but it can come up occasionally, so now you'll know to check for it.

The more you practice, the more proficient you will become at asking quality questions. You will see evidence of this as you produce more reliable answers, with fewer **need more info** responses.

Next we'll move into special uses for pendulums. This is where the real "mojo" happens.

CHAPTER FOUR:
MOJO AND SPECIAL USES

Multiple-Choice

It is a little-known secret that the pendulum can answer multiple-choice questions. Most people who use the pendulum were taught signs for **yes** and **no,** but life doesn't always present opportunities in such simplistic format. Thankfully, the pendulum adapts.

You could draw a chart and hang the pendulum over the center of the chart and then ask it to swing toward the most optimal choice or outcome, but honestly, who has time to sketch out a chart every time a complex question arises?
Meet the multiple-choice format.

How to Designate the Choices

The first step in asking a multiple-choice question is to create the question, which includes designating choices or options. For example, let's say you and your sweetie want to go out to dinner, and you're in no mood for an endless session of "I don't know, where do you want to go?" vs. "I don't know, what do you feel like eating?" The Yemenese joint with the fabulous yak has already become passé (to be honest, we are *all* sick of hearing about it), and now you're looking for something a little less exotic. You have a few ideas, but nothing stands out from the rest. Or perhaps you're in the space called "I'm starving, can we please pick something already?"

Your easiest move in this situation is to narrow down the scope to the four basic dining out choices: Chinese, Mexican, Italian or burger joint.

None of the Above

Personally, I have no problem admitting that the Universe is way smarter than me and my little monkey brain. Because of this, I always like to include a fifth option called **none of the above.** That way, when the Universe comes up with the idea that makes me smack my forehead and ask, "Why didn't I think of that?" I've got room for it to show up in my Truth Testing.

In this classic case of "where to eat tonight?" an answer of **none of the above** could mean it's optimal to order in, have leftovers, hit the food court, pick up takeout, find a food truck, or just grab a slice on the go.

Multiple-Choice Checking

To check in on a multiple-choice question (without pen and paper), splay out the fingers of your non-dominant hand (palm-side down) on the nearest flat surface and simply "name" each finger to represent one of the choices. I'm right-handed, so I would name each finger on my left hand by touching it lightly and saying or thinking each option.

With our dining dilemma example (trust me, this comes up a lot more often than any of us want to admit), here's exactly how that would play out.

With my right index finger, I lightly touch my left pinkie and say or think, "Chinese food." Then I touch my left ring finger and say or think, "Mexican," then touch my left middle finger and say or think, "Italian," and then touch my left index finger and say or think, "burger joint," and then touch my left thumb and say or think, "none of the above."

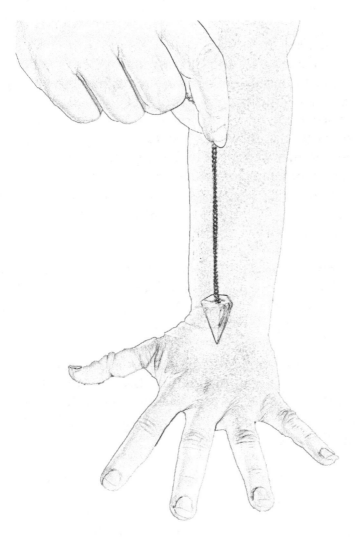

Figure 2.
Recommended hand position for multiple choice.

Next, I hold my pendulum with my right hand (the hand I write with) so that it dangles over the middle of my left hand. This way, it is free to swing toward the most optimal option/finger. My fingers are spread widely so that I can clearly see which answer the pendulum is showing me.

NOTE: If you are left-handed, you will assign the options to the fingers of your right hand. It does not matter whether you designate your thumb or pinkie as **none of the above** but I do recommend that you pick one and stick with it, because it makes it easier to remember the other choices going forward. I like to use my thumb, since it's separate and distinct from the other fingers. Remember that old Sesame Street song? "One of these things is not like the others. One of these things just doesn't belong." Good. Now it's stuck in your head, too. May it serve you well and help you remember which finger you've designated as none of the above.

As you dangle the pendy, you can ask along these lines: "All things considered, which is the most optimal option?" If you like, you can get more specific: "All things considered, which is the most optimal place for us to eat tonight?"

Yes, I know. When you're hungry or tired, it's kind of a bitch to see that **none of the above** option, because it sort of feels like you have to go back to the drawing board. But don't fret; when that happens, set down your pendulum for a minute and ask yourself this question:

"If I could ___ anything (or anywhere), what (or where) would I really want to _____?"

In the case of our culinary quandary, you might ask: "If I could eat anything right now, what would I really love to eat?" and this will likely give you the answer that is most optimal (which of course you can verify with Truth Testing). Problem solved; tummy happy.

Before Ingesting

Multiple-choice testing is useful for a lot more than just deciding where to eat. Have you ever found yourself taking a pill or supplement, yet wondering whether or not it was really working? Now you can know for sure, *before* you buy that über-expensive bottle or prescription. Are you wondering whether or not it's dairy that's giving you such foul intestinal troubles? Suspicious of the side effects of one substance or another? Curious about how that third glass of wine will really affect you? Read on and learn.

Many years ago, Marilyn Overcast taught me this simple trick for testing any substance before you ingest it.

Position your hands in the same manner I just explained for multiple-choice (as pictured on page 61), with one exception: name your fingers the following (can start with thumb or pinkie; it doesn't matter):

Medicinal ❖ Beneficial ❖ Neutral ❖ Detrimental ❖ Toxic

Then, just as you did for a multiple-choice question, hold the pendulum over the center of your hand, and ask: "All things considered, what is the effect of [name of substance] on my body?"

I can't tell you how much money I've saved and how many multi-level-marketing products I've escaped buying because of this one simple technique. Certainly, if something has a detrimental or toxic effect on your body, you want to find an alternative.* But if the effect is neutral, then you are literally flushing that substance (plus whatever you paid for it) down the toilet. If the effect is beneficial or medicinal, then it makes sense to keep investing in and using that substance.

*NOTE: I am not a physician and I will not advise you regarding your medication. I am teaching you to take your health back into your own hands and to work with your energetic team and your guides to determine the most optimal path to your wellness.

Please consult a medical professional if you are considering stopping any prescription drugs or medication. Do your research and find out if there are natural alternatives that are just as effective. You would be wise to Truth Test these alternatives as well.

There is always a possibility that even the most natural of substances could be toxic for your body. Likewise, a prescription drug with a long list of nasty side effects may actually have an appropriately medicinal effect on your body. You are an individual. Be proactive and test for yourself, have at least one other person verify the test, and then find a solution that works for you. But please, don't quit your prescription drugs cold turkey. Generally speaking, that can have very unpleasant consequences!

Yes, you can use this Truth Testing method to check on behalf of another (friends, children, spouses, pets, etc.).

Here is a more specific example of how this can play out, (and by the way, this is my personal information. So, you know, keep it on the DL). A couple of years ago, as I was coming off a Master Cleanse, I got the clear and distinct message from my body that I had to stop eating beef because my body could not tolerate it. This kind of bummed me out, because I like a good ribeye now and then, and who doesn't love a thick and juicy burger? But the message was clear: *stop eating beef.* My friends tried to console me, "Oh, I'm sure it just means to cut back on beef. If you eat it now and then, make sure it's well-raised and grass-fed, and you'll be fine." But even then I knew I was all done with beef of any kind. Incidentally, this came on the heels of my wanting to get into alignment with my body and to create a mutually respectful relationship. I decided if my body made a request, I was going to do my best to honor it, and consequently, myself. This one small shift has served me well, and I honestly do not miss beef, at all.

In a related story, I have friends who swear that you cannot be in total spiritual alignment if you eat pig. They try to convince me to stop eating pork because they claim that piggies are filthy animals, and that enlightened beings all agree we should not consume pork. In my head, I just look at God and shrug, because bacon is so damn tasty. I could honestly become a vegan if not for eggs and pigs. I don't care if "all the other enlightened ones" are passing on the pork, I'll eat their share and they can have all the grass-fed cows I'll never eat.

Sugar is another substance that gets a bad rap across the board. If you've heard me speak, you've probably heard me talk about the fact that I used to have a sugar addiction. Not anymore. I cleared it, and I've cleared all sorts of addictions for many others. Sugar is not bad; it's our relationship with sugar that needs retooling. Granted, some people do not tolerate it well (and not just diabetics, either) and if you want to know where you stand with sugar, you would be wise to test and see what effect it has on your body.

The kind of sugar makes a difference, so keep that in mind. Cane sugar, coconut sugar, corn syrup, honey, soda, beet sugar, molasses, sucralose, fructose, stevia, and agave are all different and can have very different effects on the body. Lots of naturopaths swear by stevia because the artificial sweeteners are supposedly so toxic for you. And yet, one of my friends has a horrible sensitivity to stevia. For her, stevia rates "detrimental." For me, sucralose rates "neutral," but for others, it's a clear "toxic." Are you beginning to see why it pays to check in? It's the only way you'll know for certain what's good for you and what's creating an adverse reaction in your body.

Here's an example. I do not tolerate pastries very well. For me, there's something about the combination of sugar and gluten that doesn't play nice within my body. I can tolerate occasional wheat with no problem, as long as I keep it varied (sandwich bread today, waffle tomorrow, turkey pot pie the next day, English muffin the following day, etc.) but **wheat+sugar=no bueno** for me. How do you think I discovered this? Through observation and Truth Testing. I don't eat a lot of sugar, but my body craves dark chocolate, especially when I'm writing. Which reminds me. I'll, um, be right back.

There, that's better. Moving on... root beer is actually a *spiritual* food for me. I don't crave it very often but when I do, I can drink quite a bit of it without any repercussions. I am fairly certain if I were to drink it more often than I do, there would be consequences, in which case it might rate poorly on my five-finger test. But for now it works quite well and I feel as though it fills my soul as it fills my mouth. Mmm, I love root beer!

A root beer float would really hit the spot, but only if it's made with coconut ice cream or almond milk ice cream, and not with any cow's milk product. And definitely no whipped cream. Ugh. That makes my stomach churn just to think about it! My body cannot tolerate whipped cream or sour cream at all, not even a smidge, and ice cream made from cow's milk is just as bad.

Why am I telling you all about the things I can and cannot eat?

Because the above is still true for me today, and you can actually use these questions to check in on my behalf.

Take a minute now to test the following questions. Use the five-finger technique with the substance effect labels (medicinal, beneficial, neutral, detrimental, and toxic), and jot down the answers you get. The correct answers follow this exercise so that you can verify what you got as true.

1. All things considered, what is the effect of beef on Amy's body?

2. All things considered, what is the effect of grass-fed beef on Amy's body?

3. All things considered, what is the effect of pork on Amy's body?

4. All things considered, what is the effect of bacon on Amy's body?

5. All things considered, what is the effect of sucralose on Amy's body?

6. All things considered, what is the effect of dark chocolate on Amy's body?

7. All things considered, what is the effect of occasional root beer on Amy's body?

8. All things considered, what is the effect of sour cream on Amy's body?

9. All things considered, what is the effect of whipped cream on Amy's body? (not in a kinky way)

10. All things considered, what is the effect of yak meat on Amy's body?

Once you've written down all your answers, you can flip ahead to find the actual answers. Before you do, consider some of the benefits of Truth Testing the effects of various substances on your body:

❖ It helps to know which foods make you sick or uncomfortable.

❖ You can decide whether you're getting your money's worth for those designer vitamins or rare and expensive rain forest-derived supplements.

❖ You can order meals in a way that even the chef hadn't considered (forget "on the side," we're going substitutions-crazy!).

❖ Just before a big date, interview, presentation, workshop, etc., you can know what not to eat in order to avoid any embarrassing intestinal distress.

❖ You can feel better knowing whether something you're taking is actually working.

❖ You can test your kids to see what's optimal for their little bodies, and in what doses (because some children require much smaller doses than what is recommended on the package).

❖ Same goes for your parents, your pets, or any person or animal under your care.

❖ It explains why Bob never has a second cup of your coffee.

❖ It now makes sense why you can't eat restaurant stew without getting sick, but you can eat Nana's stew with no problem. Well, it makes sense once you find out that Nana uses rice flour to coat the meat and potato starch to thicken the stew, but the restaurant uses wheat flour to coat the meat and corn starch to thicken the stew. (Oh, and by the way, the restaurant also uses yak meat.)

❖ You can tell the difference between an emotional craving (stress eating) vs. a legitimate physical craving that indicates your body needs particular minerals or nutrients.

❖ You no longer have to take your hippie friend's word for it when she tries to convince you that eggs (or gluten or store-bought juice) are the antichrist.

❖ You can also empower your children to check for themselves, which is the ultimate defense against peer pressure. "No thanks, weed just doesn't agree with my body."

Sometimes we are afraid to know because we'd prefer to stay

in denial. We think that knowing means we will have to give up that food or substance forever. That's the same reason I waited years to do anything about my known sugar addiction. I loved sugar! I didn't want to give it up, and I was certain that's what had to happen. But that's not true. Like any other block, an addiction can be cleared.

This book is not about clearing addictions, so I'll leave that topic for another time. Let's just say that if you know what foods you can't tolerate, you are then empowered to make informed choices whenever you eat. This means you can choose to skip it, you can consciously choose to eat it with the understanding that consequences are on the way, or you can be proactive and find a reasonable substitute that works with your body (rating at the very least, neutral). Of course, you can also take it one step further and clear the sensitivity. Have you read my book, *1-2-3 Clarity?*

Look to the next page for the answers to the testing exercise.

Here are the answers to my five-finger test check-in, which you can use to double-check the answers you got:

1. toxic

2. detrimental

3. generally between beneficial and neutral. Depends on the quality of pork, and the cut. I'd count this one as correct if you came up with either beneficial or neutral.

4. beneficial

5. neutral

6. neutral

7. beneficial

8. toxic

9. toxic (again, not in a kinky way)

10. neutral (really?) I've actually eaten yak. Tastes like a wilder version of beef.

If you want to calculate your accuracy, just start with 100% and then subtract 10% for each incorrect answer. Keep in mind, your score on this exercise doesn't necessarily represent your overall accuracy score, but at least it gives you an idea of how you're doing with Truth Testing so far.

Keep practicing and your accuracy rate will continue to rise.

Restaurant Fun

By this point, you may be beginning to think I'm obsessed with food. If so, congratulations on that intuitive hit—because I am. I'm a foodie who was born and raised in New Orleans, and when I moved to Colorado after Hurricane Katrina, I had to learn to cook (seriously, the food in Colorado is completely meh). We became Food Network addicts and by the age of three, my kids could recognize and name all the celeb chefs. Now I love to cook and I enjoy taking professional culinary classes to surprise myself and my family with new tasty concoctions.

To me, food is more than a necessary tool for sustaining life. It is a social staple, a creative caper, and a venue through which I express myself and experience the flavors of the Divine. If you happen to be one of those rare people who "doesn't care much about food" then you can feel free to take all of my food examples in this book and think of something else, like... wait, I can't think of anything else that is as universal as food. Well, I'm sure you'll think of something with all that free time you must have while you're not thinking about food. Meanwhile, the rest of us are going to talk about food some more.

Want to have great fun the next time you visit a restaurant? Use your pendulum to order from the menu!

I have noticed that people have different ways of deciding what to order when dining out. Take a look at these examples and notice which ones sound most like you:

❖ You've got a hankering for something in particular, so you choose the restaurant based on its ability to rock that dish.

- ❖ You order based on photos, as in a Thai or sushi or Indian restaurant.

- ❖ You pick whatever is fastest, because time is of the essence or you're very hungry.

- ❖ You choose based on price, sometimes depending on who's paying for the meal.

- ❖ You pick the biggest portion, either because you are very hungry, or you like to get a good value, or you want leftovers for lunch tomorrow.

- ❖ You select what sounds good right now; whatever strikes your fancy.

- ❖ You order your favorite dish, or you order the same thing whenever you go to this particular place.

- ❖ You order a dish that can be shared.

- ❖ You choose based on dietary restrictions, like gluten-free, vegetarian/vegan, nut-free, or what could be easily modified to suit your preferences.

- ❖ You pick something light or healthy, like a salad or something fresh.

- ❖ You get the dish with the most of something you want, like veggies or meat or cheese (or bacon).

- ❖ You select a dish you've always wanted to try.

- ❖ You choose something you haven't eaten in awhile.

❖ You pick the dish that seems to jump off the page as you skim the menu.

❖ You make your final choice between two entrees based on what your dinner companion is *not* ordering (in hopes of sharesies).

What kind of selection process best suits you? Personally, I'm more of a "what jumps out at me" kind of girl, but I wasn't always that way. I used to be very analytical about deciding what to order, and a lot of times, I was disappointed with what I got. Once I decided to let myself be guided into choosing, I was surprised and delighted at what I wound up eating!

We tried this experiment once with a finicky eater. Several of us went out to a Mexican restaurant, and this picky friend decided to be brave and let her trusty pendy decide. She wound up ordering calamari, which she was alarmed to discover was deep-fried squid. The dish was gorgeously plated, as the calamari rested on a fresh spinach salad. The calamari was cut into rings from the body; not the tentacles, which is the part I prefer. Her eyes were big as saucers as the waiter placed the dish in front of her. We all stared and held our breath as she took the first bite.

Success! She loved it. The spinach was tossed with a very acidic dressing, which complemented the squid perfectly. She ate every bite and was blown away at how well her pendy had served her. Watching her experience, everyone at the table vowed to use Truth Testing to select their restaurant meals from now on.

Honestly, I don't always check in with my pendulum to decide what to eat. Sometimes I have a hankering for something in particular, and that's what my taste buds are set on. Most of the time, I glance through the menu and one or two things will seem to leap off the page at me. That's when I'll use the pendulum to pick a winner between those options, and from time to time, it means I order something I never would have thought twice about otherwise. I continue to be surprised and delighted at what I am guided to order. Here's how to do it.

It all starts with an open mind. I promise you, if you are dreading using your pendulum to choose your meal, terrified that it will swing toward the thing you hate most of all, then that's probably what will happen. Resistance is a powerful force, even when it comes to something as pleasurable as food. Begin with an open mind and the thought that you can relax and trust that whatever is chosen for you will be delightful. It's not all yak! If you always order chicken, you might be inspired to order a pork or vegetarian dish instead, or a chicken dish that's prepared in a way you've never tried. You will nearly always be overjoyed that you were open and you listened. And if the dish is not enjoyable, then know that you have permission from the Universe to send it back and order the Cobb salad instead. Of course, then you'll have to use your pendulum to choose a dressing....

Once your mind is open, there are a couple of different ways to check in, and while they both work, the one you should use is largely dependent upon the size of the menu. With a small menu, you can just hold your pendulum over the menu and ask it to swing toward the most optimal thing for you to eat, then keep adjusting until it's directly over the thing you will order. For example, if a one-page menu features appetizers, salads, and sandwiches, then you can hold your pendulum over the middle of the page and see which way it swings. If it swings down toward sandwiches, then you can reposition the pendy so it's suspended over the middle of the sandwich section. Then ask again and see which sammie it swings toward. Let's say that turns out to be the Reuben (my mother's favorite). Then you can verify by holding your pendulum normally (not over the menu) and ask, "ATC, is it optimal for me to get a Reuben?" If **no,** look at what's near Reuben on the menu, as you may have slightly misread the swing.

Alternatively, if the menu is rather large and tri-fold you can do it this way. (By the way, why do Mexican restaurants always have colossal menus? Thank goodness they are kind enough to give me chips and salsa to munch on as I speed-read this novella of a menu.)

Open the menu and lay it flat. Ask your pendulum to swing toward the page that contains what is optimal for you to eat (left, center, or right). If the menu is longer than a tri-fold (for example, an eight-page menu. Why oh why did you pick Mexican again?), then turn the pages one by one and ask the pendy to remain still until you get to the page that contains your most optimal dish. Repeat until you have gone through the entire menu, as it may be optimal for you to order more than one item (a salad and an entree, or a couple of apps and dessert perhaps).

Once you know which page you are ordering from, follow the one-page menu instructions above, or use your fingers for multiple-choice categories (starter, salad, soup, side dish, etc.). Once you've identified the category, you can either hold your pendulum over the center of that category and ask it to swing toward the most optimal item, or you can use your fingers for multiple-choice. Finish by asking for verification that you've selected the most optimal item. (All things considered, is the yak brisket the most optimal dish for me?)

This may sound like a lot, but I promise you it goes quickly.

The first time, it might take you four or five minutes to order (and let's face it, that may be on par with how long you usually take to order), but after that it goes very fast.

If you're worried about whipping out a pendulum in the middle of a restaurant, read the section called **The Body Sway** in Chapter 7, which explains how to use your body as a pendulum. This comes in handy when you'd like to be less conspicuous. But honestly, I use a pendulum in restaurants all the time and the most I've ever gotten from the waiter is curious interest and perhaps a couple of questions (at which point, I typically give them a link to my YouTube videos). As a general rule, people are too engrossed in themselves to even notice you using a pendulum, so there's no need to feel self-conscious about it.

Traveling Assistance

I don't know about you, but I love to travel and I do it every chance I get. When travel is smooth, it's delightful. But when it's not, there's nothing worse than being plagued with unexpected delays, cancelled flights, road construction, horrific weather, or lost reservations. But what's a frequent flyer to do? There's far too much world left to see, so we can't be expected to just stay home, right?

Good news. While you can't always predict the future (though meteorologists have tried for decades), you **can** put yourself in a position to create the best possible outcome when traveling, simply by using Truth Testing to check in before you make your plans.

Wondering if it really makes a difference? After all, shouldn't you just take the redeye, or the nonstop, or the flight with the lowest fare, or the one on your favorite airline, or the one with the upgrade option? You are certainly free to do that. But you are also free to check in and see what is most optimal, and then expect to be delighted by the Universe.

Here are a few examples of what I've experienced once I began to check in before making any travel plans.

On a very long flight from Denver, Colorado to Sydney, Australia, there were so few people on the plane that each of the five of us had a whole row of seats in which to lie down and sleep. Too bad I didn't check in before I picked which movie to watch. Remember that Jodie Foster flick where she falls asleep on the airplane and someone steals her kid and the flight crew pretends her kid was never on the flight at all? Yeah, *don't* watch that one before you fly halfway around the world with your kids. I didn't sleep a wink, even though my nine-month-old slept nearly the entire flight. But I digress. The point is that of all the flights between Denver and Sydney, and of all the days I could have chosen to fly, the one my pendulum helped me pick is the one that gave us plenty of space to stretch and (for all of us except me) to sleep. I asked the flight attendant if this was typical for such a flight at this time of day. "Oh goodness no," she said. "This flight is always jam-packed. Looks like you got lucky."

Here's another example. Just recently, I was planning a writer's retreat for myself. I wanted to get away someplace close by and lovely, and since it was just before Christmas and shortly after we had bought and furnished a new home, I wanted to keep the expense low. Basically, I wanted a champagne getaway on a beer budget. No sooner had I set that intention then we got an email with a discount code for our favorite local luxury resort, just forty-five minutes from home. Since we are proudly a one-car family, I knew I would need to rent a car so that I could drive myself there and back.

However, I was unable to book the car online. Every time I tried to prepay the reservation online, something would go wrong and double the price. I even called the car rental company, but they couldn't explain it. Frustrated, I checked in and got it wasn't optimal to book the car, so I figured I'd just do it later. Within the hour, my writing compadre saw my "Yay! I'm taking myself on a writer's retreat" post on Facebook and asked if I wanted company. Yes, as a matter of fact I did. She booked herself a room straight away and guess what? Since I'm on her way there, she offered to pick me up and drive me home. "Unless you wanted to bring your own car," she said. Ha! Are you kidding? Did I mention I hate driving?

Also, a few days after I booked the resort, I found out my daughter got a part in the school play, which was scheduled to run the night I got back. Had I not checked in before booking the resort, I might have missed the play entirely, or had to make costly changes to my itinerary in order to be back in time. Because I checked in, it all synchronized perfectly.

By using Truth Testing to plan and book travel, I have avoided road construction, gridlock traffic, and bad weather on road trips; I've picked hotels with super-friendly management who comp'd us all kinds of extras (including free in-room movies); and I've somehow managed to visit the busiest of tourist places during inexplicable lulls.

Here's how you do it:

Don't take anything for granted, and check in on all the details before you commit.

Let's take a look at how this might play out in a real world scenario. For this example, let's say your friend Marcy in Boston (Maaahhhcie in Baaaahhston) calls you up and invites you to come for a visit next month. "That sounds wicked awesome," you say. "Let me mull it over and get back with you." Here is a list of the questions you might ask:

- ❖ **All things considered (ATC), is it optimal for me to go to Boston?** If no, you could check the surrounding towns, but more than likely, it's not optimal to take the trip.

- ❖ **ATC, is it optimal for me to visit Marcy?** Again, if you get no, you're pretty much done. You could check and see if there's a better time of year to visit, but for now, it's a no-go. The rest of the questions assume you've received a yes for taking this trip.

- ❖ **ATC, is next month the most optimal time for me to visit?** If not, then when?

- ❖ **ATC, is it optimal for me to stay with Marcy?** If not, then where? You could use multiple-choice to check hotel, B&B, timeshare, homeless shelter, etc.

- ❖ **ATC, is it optimal for me to fly into Boston?** This may seem like an obvious yes if you live far away, like L.A., but maybe Logan Airport in Boston is not the most optimal option. Perhaps you are to tour the New England area during this trip, which might mean flying into New Hampshire, Connecticut, or Vermont. Take nothing for granted and check in on everything.

- ❖ **ATC, what is the most optimal day for me to fly into Boston?** I like to use the multiple-choice option for this, starting with which week is optimal to fly there, and then narrowing it down to a specific day. Once I've decided when I'm flying out, I use the pendulum to determine the optimal number of days for the trip to last, and then confirm which day is optimal for me to fly back (because it's possible that it's optimal to fly elsewhere after Boston).

❖ **ATC, is it optimal to fly nonstop?** If you get need more info that may mean it doesn't matter. We fly nonstop whenever we take the kids, and I prefer to fly nonstop when I fly alone; however, sometimes the cost savings for a two-leg trip is astronomical, and if I'm flying solo I just might do it.

This is usually the point where I'll hop on Travelocity or some other travel website to check the fares and my time options for departure and arrival. There may be some factors to consider, such as whether or not your friend is picking you up at the airport, and what time they are able to do so. Or you may need to consider your travel companions' sleep schedule, or heavy traffic times, or nap times for the kids.

Likewise, you don't want to take the redeye if it means sitting at the airport for three hours waiting for your friend to pick you up.

Once those considerations are addressed, you can usually narrow down your options to just a few scant choices. (Incidentally, I also check in to see whether it's optimal to purchase via Travelocity or direct from the airline's website.)

Of note, the pendulum does not always select the least expensive flight. I'd rather not take what feels like an overpriced flight, but I'm happy to pay something in the low- or midrange if that's what pendy advises. Trust me, taking the cheapest flight does not always get you the best experience. It can mean lost luggage, extended delays, cranky flight crews, wailing babies, or worst of all—getting bumped off an overbooked flight. Same goes for hotels. Which brings us to our next question.

❖ **ATC, is it optimal to buy travel insurance? I'm** amazed at how often the answer is no but it doesn't hurt to ask. Of course, if you have some uncertainty in your life (your partner is expecting a baby, your job requires you to be available on the fly, you have health issues, or you're booking a cruise during hurricane season) then by all means, just buy the dang trip insurance without checking in. The peace of mind you'll get is worth the relatively few bucks you'll spend. But if life is good and you don't see any reason why you wouldn't take that trip, then check with pendy regarding the optional insurance.

❖ Once you've got the travel dates and you're ready to pull the trigger on the booking (whether that means paying the deposit for the cruise, buying the airfare, or prepaying that rental car), then this is the key question to ask: **ATC, is it optimal to book/pay for this now?** If you get **no,** do yourself a favor and wait. Remember my writer's retreat? Imagine how ticked I would have been if I had prepaid $120 for a rental car and then discovered I had a ride offer from my friend. I'm delighted that my highest self was smart enough to create those computer glitches so that I didn't book it when I wanted to (because while I had checked in and it was optimal to book the resort, I had not checked in about the car rental before I started trying to book it. Doh!).

If you get yes and everything feels good, do it. Don't delay or you will wind up missing an opportunity to have a great trip at a great price.

If you get wonky answers, have someone else check for you (preferably not Marcy, as she may have a bias), or try again later. Sometimes something needs to shift or new information needs to appear before it's the optimal time to plan your travel.

I realize this may seem like a lengthy process, but it all moves rather quickly once you've been through it once, and the results are definitely worth it. How long does it take you without Truth Testing to book a flight and make decisions like these? With the pendulum, it should take the same amount of time or less. Plus, when you factor in all the time you'll save by avoiding potential delays and hassles, you'll be glad you invested in checking in. Happy trails!

Are They Lying to You?

Have you ever wondered if someone was telling you truth? As an intuitive, I often get hints or hunches when someone is being less than truthful. When we were dating, my dear husband could never surprise me because I always knew when he was up to something (still do, actually). I remember once he called me at work just to see how my day was going, and I could tell something was strange. Twenty minutes later, a huge floral arrangement was delivered to my desk. He had called because he wanted to know if it had arrived, and he didn't want to come out and ask, but something in his voice gave him away. Of course, the downside of knowing when secrets are afoot is that no one has ever successfully thrown me a surprise party. Oh, I know. Poor me, right?

But perhaps you have not been so fortunate. Maybe you've had the unpleasant experience of finding out that someone in your life has been lying to you through their teeth for some time now. It feels like a kick in the gut to experience that kind of betrayal, and you might feel as though some part of you should have known, that you somehow should have seen it coming. You look back and in hindsight, realize all the signs you must have missed along the way.

Now you have a way to check in and see what's going on if you have the sneaking suspicion that things aren't as they seem. The question is simple, as long as you keep it focused on the information, and not the person.

Look, if you think your boss Jerry knows about some upcoming layoffs, and yet he's dodging your questions about the matter, it's important that you ask about the layoffs, and not about Jerry.

If you ask, "ATC, is Jerry telling me the truth?" you could get a **no** even if he is being truthful in his vague responses to your direct questions. Let's face it, if it's true, then Jerry is probably concerned with saving his own ass right now, and who can blame him? Besides which, even if your job is safe, Jerry can't go around telling some employees about the layoffs and expect them to keep it a secret from the ones who are about to get the axe. Jerry's got to be discreet until the time has come to make the official announcements. But just because Jerry needs to toe the corporate line, that doesn't mean you have to sit idly by and wait for the news to drop.

Instead, you could ask: "Is it true and accurate that the company is currently planning layoffs?" or "ATC, is my job in jeopardy?" or "ATC, is it optimal for me to update my résumé?" or "ATC, is it optimal for me to schedule a meeting with human resources to discuss a transfer?" If you suspect some restructuring is imminent at your workplace, I would also recommend checking in before making any major purchases in your personal life, especially anything on credit (although to be honest, that's good advice even if your job isn't in danger. But more about that later in this book).

Got Kids? This form of truth testing is also helpful in sorting out sibling arguments over what they did or didn't do. When your kids play the "it wasn't me" card, you can actually take out a pendulum and check to see whether or not that's true. "ATC, who broke the vase?" or "ATC, who made a mess of the kitchen?" or "ATC, who took the $20 out of my wallet?"

I recommend showing your children how to use a pendulum, so that they can see the accuracy of it first-hand. Once my kids saw the power of Truth Testing, I only had to threaten to pull out a pendulum before someone 'fessed up. Imagine my folded arms and furrowed brow as I tap my feet and say in a stern voice, "Kids, do I need to check with the pendulum to see who is telling the truth?" Within seconds, one head would hang low, followed by a sigh, and then a quiet voice owns an admission of guilt. (As a parent, it's wise to try not to look too smug when this happens.)

There is one caveat to using a pendulum to determine whether or not someone is lying to you, and this is related to **infidelity.** I have noticed something curious over the years in working with countless clients and students: when a person suspects his or her life partner of being unfaithful, it is very difficult for that person to get a clear and accurate answer. Usually, this is because the person feels triggered or activated by old betrayals, which may or may not be from the person they are currently committed to, and may or may not have happened in this lifetime. The old betrayal takes over, and fear and paranoia start driving the bus, making it hard to get a clear answer with the pendulum.

In these cases, it is best to have an objective third party verify the answer. Remember, there is no need to air your dirty laundry or verbalize the question to this kind and innocent volunteer. Rather, hold the question silently in your mind ("ATC, did [name] cheat on me?") and ask the other person to check in to see whether the answer to the question in your mind is **yes** or **no**.

Incidentally, "cheat" is one of those words that leaves a lot up to interpretation. What does cheating mean to you? What counts as cheating: sex, kissing, fantasizing, impure thoughts, or flirting? You can get as specific as you want as you ask these questions, because the objective third-party won't know what the questions are if you keep them silent.

If you find yourself doubting the verification, ask two more individuals to verify for you (be sure to keep the question exactly the same each time) and look for unanimous answers across the board. If the answer is **yes**, I'm sorry you had to hear that. You are now faced with the decision whether or not to confront your partner and what to do next.

Wow. This chapter has taken a bit of a downward turn, I'm afraid. Let's move on to more inspiring uses for the pendulum, shall we?

Finding Lost Items

The pendulum is also useful for finding lost items. Here are two easy ways you can use Truth Testing to locate something you've lost. It helps to have a general idea of where the item may be (for example, lost in your house somewhere or on your property).

The first method requires your presence onsite. With your

pendulum in hand, begin by confirming whether or not the object is in fact located in the building or space. You might ask, "Is it true and accurate that the [missing object] is here in this [building; property; car; house; whatever is appropriate to describe the space]?" Next, systematically walk the space and ask, "Is the [object] in this room?" If you get **no,** move to the next room, and continue until you get a **yes.** Once you get a **yes,** you can stand in the center of that room or area and ask your trusty pendy to swing toward the location of the object in question. If the room or space is very large, you might prefer to divide it into quadrants, then you can move from quadrant to quadrant asking "Is it true and accurate that the missing object is in this part of the room?" Continue narrowing the space until you've pinpointed the location of the missing object.

The other method is similar, yet it does not require you to be present in the space itself. Obtain or draw a simple map of the space in question. Don't stress yourself out over this, okay? A CAD drawing to scale isn't necessary; the map can be a simple mock-up sketched with pencil and paper. Begin by using the pendulum to verify the lost item is in the space represented by the map. Then you can either hold your pendulum over the center of the paper and ask it to swing toward the item's location, or you can hold your pendy over one area at a time and ask if it's true and accurate that the item is in this area. Continue narrowing down the space until you have pinpointed the exact location.

BONUS POINTS: As an added measure, I like to begin either of these processes by picturing the item as found, instead of fixating on the fact that it's lost. Florence Scovel Shinn said, "There is no loss in Divine Mind," and I find it helps to affirm that statement while I look for the item. This shifts my energy out of stress, loss, and fear, and into a space of relaxed confidence, thereby facilitating a smoother search with a higher probability of a successful find.

If you are unsuccessful at finding your lost item, it may be optimal to cut your losses and buy a replacement (or let it go and do without). Which brings us to our next special use for the pendulum: **money.**

Money Maturity

This next method is one of my all-time favorite applications for the pendulum, and I have recommended it to many clients and students with amazing results. If you want to transform your relationship with money, this is the perfect exercise for you.

For the next seven days, use your pendulum to ask two questions before you spend any money. I'm talking about any amount at all—even a five-dollar Starbucks. Yes, it sounds like a pain in the ass, but that's only because it is. But it's just for a week and I promise if you do this, it will begin to transform your relationship with the big M.

The first question is:

All things considered, is it optimal for me to have this?

The second question is:

Does money want to go here?

If you get **no** to the first question, you're done. Sorry, you're not getting it today. If you get a **yes** to the first question, then proceed with the second question. Do not proceed with the purchase (no matter how trivial) unless the answer to both questions is **yes.**

The purpose of question #1 is to determine whether or not the thing belongs in your possession. Question #2 determines the **where** and **when** aspect of the equation.

You may be wondering why a person would get **yes** to the first question and **no** to the second. Perhaps it's optimal for you to have the thing (or experience) but it's not optimal to spend money here because:

❖ Someone will gift it to you.

❖ You will win it in a contest or prize drawing.

❖ It will go on sale later.

❖ You will find a coupon or other form of significant savings.

❖ Your money is needed more elsewhere (e.g., a local shop instead of a big box store; a place with nicer sales personnel or a better return policy; etc.).

❖ You will find something better for the same (or better) price.

This exercise is likely to piss you off at least once during the week. Let's face it, we are accustomed to instant gratification, and when we are told (even by our Highest Self) that it's not optimal to get what we want right now, our inner child is likely to stamp her feet and pout. But if you're struggling with money right now, it may be because you give in too often to these primal urges, which is exactly what we're looking to shift.

In the same vein, sometimes you will expect to get **no** to the first question when asking about a purchase that is not necessary, at least not right now, and you may be surprised to find the answer is a **yes.**

Must you listen and obey? That's up to you. After all, free will reigns supreme. You don't even have to do this exercise if you don't want to. The two-question exercise is designed to show you what's optimal; whether or not you take that advice is up to you. But if you do, here are a few of the benefits you can expect to gain as a result of doing this activity for one full week:

❖ greater maturity with money

❖ little to no buyer's remorse

❖ improved relationship with money overall

❖ greater trust in the Universe

❖ increased wisdom with money

❖ smarter spending

❖ more discipline with money

❖ less subject to the "gimmies" and "gotta haves"

❖ spending within your means

❖ reduced attachment to material possessions

❖ openness to miracles and ways to receive without spending

If you do the exercise, drop me a line and tell me about your experience, I'd love to hear from you.

CHAPTER FIVE:
BIAS AND THIRD PARTY
VERIFICATION

Bias, Preference, and Attachment

The question I get asked the most often is whether or not a person can influence the pendulum's answers. To which I respond, "Hell yes!" If you have a strong preference or attachment one way or another, you are **biased,** which means you can definitely swing the pendulum in a certain direction without consciously intending to. Since the whole point of Truth Testing is to get a true and accurate answer, it's worth taking a few minutes here to learn how to avoid the influence of bias.

How does bias show up? Sometimes it's obvious, like when we know we want a certain answer. Other times, the answer might appear suspect, and you think, "Hmm, it's saying **yes** but I'm not so sure." Or you may see inconsistency in the answers when multiple people check in and get conflicting responses. These are all good indicators that bias is present.

Here are several ways you can handle bias when it shows up:

❖ Ask your question, then say, **"Please show me a clear and unbiased answer."** This works for most people, but not everyone. It's worth a shot to see if it works for you, as this is the easiest method of all.

❖ If I know I have a bias before I ask, I will often begin by asking, **"Am I able to get an unbiased answer on this right now?"** If that answer is **no,** then I'll ask later or seek out a third-party verification. If I get **yes,** it seems to suspend my bias long enough to get a reliable answer.

❖ **Begin by swinging your pendulum in a way that is <u>not</u> one of your signs.** For example, if your signs are universal, then you might swing it around in a circle. Close your eyes and hold the question in your mind. Sit for a few seconds, and then open your eyes to see an unbiased answer. This is my husband's favorite method for asking when he knows he has a bias (or when I accuse him of having one).

❖ If the answer seems suspect, you can ask, **"Is that a true and unbiased answer?"** Nine times out of ten, you'll get a **no** if bias is present. When this happens, this is a good time to call in third party verification. If they get a different answer from yours, you can bet you're the one who's biased, at which point it helps to call in **another** third party verification as tiebreaker.

❖ **Distract yourself** by asking your question and then close your eyes and think of something totally different, but not another question. For example, if you ask, "ATC, is it optimal for me to go to the movies tonight?" then you might distract yourself by thinking about what you had for breakfast, or trying to recall what Great Aunt Josephine sent you for your birthday last year. **HINT:** it was probably a card and a check. Did you call and thank her? By the time you bring your attention back, you can open your eyes and see your uninfluenced answer.

❖ If I know I have a strong bias, **I will sometimes distract myself by thinking of my next move if I get the answer I don't want.** For example, if I really want to get a **yes,** I'll ask my question and then look away and think about what I will do next if the answer is **no.** This helps to lessen my attachment as I focus on alternative solutions. As a bonus, if I get the answer I don't want, it's no big deal because I've detached from needing it to go a certain way, and I've already thought of a suitable solution. Win-win!

I recommend trying all of the above methods to see which one you like best. I'm a big fan of whatever works.

Have Someone Else Check

At times, it is useful to have someone else verify your answers, to ensure no bias is present. While I always recommend **third-party verification** in cases of suspected infidelity, it's actually useful to have someone check for you in many other situations, including anywhere you don't trust yourself to get an honest, unbiased answer. Here are some basic guidelines for third-party verification.

Step 1: Establish Reliability and Trust

Ensure the other person knows how to use a pendulum with high reliability. You might accomplish this by having them verify a couple of answers to questions you already know the answer to, or you might already be aware that this person is handy with a pendy. I recommend having two or three people who can verify answers for you. That way, you've got a backup if you need a quick answer and the first person you reach out to isn't available when you need them. Plus, it comes in handy if you ever need a tiebreaker. If you've got no one in your life that can verify for you, pick a couple of friends and send them to my Truth Testing videos so they can learn. **http://InfoYesNo.com** Or better yet, gift them each a copy of this book... and a custom pendulum. You like your friends, right?

Step 2: Hold the question in your mind.

There is no need to say the question out loud, and you will typically find you get more reliable verification when you keep the question silent. This way, the other person cannot be biased by the question itself, your tone, or your intention when you state the question. Plus that way, you get to keep the question private. Because nobody wants to admit if they're having someone check "All things considered, is it optimal for me to eat this entire pint of Talenti?" (If it's the sea salt caramel flavor, I'm amazed you could stop long enough to check in. Mmmmm, yummy.) Remember to use good form in asking your question (only one variable, begin with "all things considered," no predictions, etc.). Let the other person know what kind of answer you are looking for, such as **yes/no** or multiple-choice **A/B/C/none of the above.**

Step 3. Say GO or OK once you've phrased the question and are ready for them to check.

Do **not** change any part of the question while they are checking, or they will get a wonky answer. Every time you change the question or any part of it, say **go** or **OK** so they know it's time to check again.

NOTE: Some people (my husband, for example) get switched signals if any of their body parts are crossed. I know it sounds weird, but the switcheroo is true. If I'm checking for him, or if he's checking for me, we both have to be uncrossed to get accurate answers. Since you won't always know if the other person switches signals if crossed, it's prudent to keep your body parts (ankles, arms, legs, eyes) uncrossed while holding the question and while they check for you.

CHAPTER SIX:
PENDULUM MYTHS & URBAN LEGENDS

Myths Dispelled

I have a confession to make. When I first put up my YouTube videos about how to use a pendulum, I did it out of sheer laziness. I was tired of talking people through the process of how to use a pendulum, so one day I figured I'd make a video and whenever someone asked me, I could just send them to the video.

Little did I know those videos would be seen by hundreds of thousands of people across the globe, or that I'd gain countless clients just by being my goofy self and doing what I love: teaching cool stuff.

However, once I put up those videos, people posted comments like crazy. Most were extremely positive and thankful, but some claimed the pendulum was nothing more than an ideomotor response, while others warned me against tools of the devil and his evil brigade. (Those people weren't amused when I asked if they had used their pendulum to check in and see whether or not that was true.)

But the comments that fascinated me the most were the myths that people wholeheartedly believe about the pendulum. In this chapter, we'll address these metaphysical urban legends and you can decide for yourself what you believe.

Myth #1: You must cleanse your pendulum regularly to ward off negative energy.

Reality: Not really. However, if you believe you must, then you must. I have actually never cleansed any of my pendulums, unless they felt dirty or slimy, in which case you can simply rinse the pendulum with water and a gentle liquid soap. If your pendulum includes natural gemstones **do not** soak it in salt water, as the salt can find its way into the natural cracks, which can cause your crystals to split.

Alternatively, you can energetically cleanse anything (stones, crystals, jewelry, pendulums) by exposing it to moonlight. Nope, it doesn't have to be a full moon or a new moon, just bright moonlight, and you don't even have to take it outdoors; you can leave it on the windowsill overnight.

Myth #2: You must cleanse a pendulum when you first get it to remove the energy of the prior owners, or anyone it's come into contact with before you.

Reality: See response above to Myth #1. However, I will say this: if you ever get a funky vibe from a pendulum, it doesn't hurt to cleanse it as described above. Better safe than sorry.

Myth #3: It's not okay to let someone else use your pendulum because the pendulum harnesses your energy, and when you let someone else use it, it mixes the messages.

Reality: Nope. At my retreats, we constantly swap up pendulums and I've never seen anyone experience diminished accuracy as a result. Having said that, I would not let someone with icky energy use my pendy, and if I did, I'd cleanse it afterwards. But then again, I don't hang out with people with icky energy, so I suppose that's a moot point. If you hang out with icky energy people, I'd say you've got bigger problems than whatever your pendy is picking up from them. Might be time to upgrade your circle of influence.

Myth #4: Some gemstones are bad for use in pendulums.

Reality: Sorry, I have to call bullshit on this one. Gemstones are awesome and one of the best substances to use in a pendulum and they all rock (pun intended). Having said that, I might not use a magnetic stone with a metal chain, but for no other reason than I can't be bothered to keep untangling the pendulum every time I want to use it.

Myth #5: My cousin said pendulums communicate with the devil.

Reality: Your cousin sounds terribly closed-minded. The pendulum is an inanimate object, which means its use is all about our intention behind it. In this work, we are accessing our Highest Self and holding the intention that all answers are sourced from that point. So unless your Highest Self happens to be Beelzebub, I'd say you're A-OK there. Maybe choose someone other than this particular cousin to be on your short list for third-party verification.

Myth #6: I'm worried about becoming hypnotized.

Reality: Nah-ah. Again, it comes down to intention. Now swing your pendulum side-to-side and repeat after me: I will buy all of Amy Scott Grant's books....

Myth #7: People will think I'm weird.

Reality: Let's be honest: if you're reading this book, you probably are weird. It's ok, we're all mad down here. Embrace your weirdness and let your freak flag fly. Liberation, baby!

Myth #8: Isn't this risky, messing around with the occult?

Reality: See response to Myth #5. Also, I'd say it's riskier to make choices based on superstition, what someone else thinks is a good idea, or what my monkey brain tells me. Life just gets better and better the more we rely on our Highest Self for guidance. If using Truth Testing is wrong, I don't wanna be right.

❖   ❖   ❖

Myth #9: It doesn't really work because if it did, I'd have won the lottery by now.

Reality: It's complicated. People ask me about lottery a lot. For some, it's the first thing they want to know when it comes to learning to use a pendulum. The thing is, there's a very strange and complex energy around gambling. Don't get me wrong; I like to hit up the slots now and then, maybe even play a little video poker, purely for entertainment. But there is a weird vibe that accompanies the energy of lottery and gambling. The simple truth is that most people have too many blocks and hang-ups around effortlessly receiving a large and sudden lump sum of money, which is the real reason it doesn't happen for most of us. But what do I know? I'm just an entrepreneur at heart. To me, it's a lot easier to go out and make the money by serving people and solving problems. Even though I do buy a Powerball ticket from time to time when the jackpot is sky-high. Can't win if you don't play, right? But just because you don't get the winning numbers with your pendulum, that doesn't mean the pendy doesn't work. Clear your blocks around winning and then see what happens.

Myth #10: I asked if such-and-such would happen, and the pendulum said yes, but it didn't happen. Why?

Reality: Because you forgot what you read in the chapter about predictions. Life is always in flux, so if you ask a prediction, know that what is **yes** or **no** in this moment may not be true five minutes from now, and in fact could change thousands of times between now and the actual occurrence. Stick to questions about what you can control in this moment, and stay away from the mind-bending predictions.

❖   ❖   ❖

Myth #11: My Wiccan friend said I can use a pendulum to cast spells.

Reality: Um, okay. I'm not Wiccan so I can't really speak to that practice. Personally, I like to stick to intentions and clearings, as I find they work very well together. Does your Wiccan friend have a spell for winning the Powerball? If so, I'd like to get her number, thanks. Strictly for research purposes, of course.

CHAPTER SEVEN:
WEIRD OTHER STUFF

If You Have More Than Three Signs

It's rare, but every once in awhile I come across someone who has more than three signs. This occurs when your pendulum moves in a way that isn't recognizable as your sign for **yes, no** or **need more info.** It shows up and you think, "WTF does *that* mean?!" If you're one of these not-so-lucky few, you'll need to play around with trial and error to see what your additional signs mean.

Here are a few examples you can test:

❖ It's not optimal to know that.

❖ Rephrase the question.

❖ Ask again later.

❖ Not right now.

Sometimes, multiple signs will normalize over time to just the three signs, which makes things far less confusing overall. Likewise, if your signs are nonstandard, they will sometimes normalize to the universal signs after some time. Once your signs normalize to the standard signs, it is unlikely that they would change again.

If You Get Conflicting Answers

When someone tells me they are getting conflicting answers, the first question I always ask them is, "Why were you asking more than once?" Sometimes I like to think of my pendy as an older, wiser sibling. One who doesn't pick on me or ask to borrow money, of course. If I ask the same question repeatedly, I may get an answer just to shut me up. How annoyed would you be if someone kept asking you the same thing over and over? How annoyed would you be if someone kept asking you the same thing over and over? How annoyed would you be if someone kept asking you the same thing over and over?

Instead of asking more than once, if you get an answer that feels goofy or "off," have someone else verify instead of asking again. You'll get a much more reliable answer that way. If the third-party verification produces conflicting results, then either rephrase your question or check to see if you have a bias.

If You Get an Answer You Know Is Wrong

What happens when you get an answer to a clear question, but you're certain it can't be correct? Besides an inherent bias, there are a few other reasons why you might get a wrong or doubtful answer to a well-phrased question.

Alcohol and/or drugs. Be advised, if you are intoxicated or otherwise under the influence, you might not be able to get reliable answers. Sleep it off, then try again when your head is clear.

Extreme fatigue or illness. When I feel crappy, whether it's from exhaustion, pain, or the common cold, I usually can't think straight, so it follows that answers wouldn't flow easily with Truth Testing. This is a good time to play the "Pooky, will you check in for me?" card and bat your eyelashes. Seriously, works every time.

Crossed signals. As I mentioned earlier, some people get switched signals when their body parts are crossed. It's not common, appearing in perhaps ten percent or fewer of the people I've worked with, but it's worth checking if you get a wonky answer. To see if you have crossed signals, simply calibrate **(yes, no, need more info)** with nothing crossed (legs, ankles, arms, fingers, eyes) and then calibrate again with your ankles crossed. If you get different answers, then you're a switcheroo and should always check with everything uncrossed. This also means when you participate in third-party verification (in either role) you and the other person should both remain uncrossed while checking.

Signals that change. It's rare, but your signals may change over time. If you're getting inconsistent answers, it doesn't hurt to recalibrate to make sure your signals are still what you think they are. Typically, I have only seen signals change when the person is fairly new to Truth Testing, and they start out with nonstandard signs. Once your signs convert to universal signs, it is extremely unlikely that they would switch again to something else. But then again, anything is possible. Calibrate to be certain.

Negative entities. I don't mean to freak you out, especially when you've stuck with me all this way into this book (thank you), but negative entities are worth mentioning. These are best described as energy parasites that can latch onto your energetic field, unbeknownst to you. Now before you go dousing yourself with energetic Lysol (ew) or perhaps Windex if you are a fan of *My Big Fat Greek Wedding,* you should know that many people have at least a couple of negative entities hanging out with them at any given time.

What I have learned is that as individuals, we have varying degrees of tolerance to these entities. In other words, I might be able to tolerate nine or ten in my field before I notice or have any adverse effects, while another person might start to feel strange with just two or three. It is highly beneficial to have your field cleaned of these entities on a regular basis, as opposed to waiting until you feel like you're going bonkers.

The reason I mention it here is this: for me, the way I know I've got too many negative entities hanging out in my field is when I get goofy answers with my pendulum. How can you tell for sure? Check in, of course. Where does one pick up such undesirable entities? It can happen easily if you are highly sensitive; are around a lot of negative people or energy on a constant basis; have been totally and completely creeped out lately; have been sick for a long while; or if you do a lot of energy work without grounding yourself beforehand and/or clearing your field afterwards.

Too close. Proximity is another reason you may get strange or unreliable answers even if the question is phrased properly. If you're too close to the person or the situation or the outcome, it can be difficult to get any clear and objective insight. This is different from bias. For example: if one of my children is sick or in pain, I have to have someone else check in for me. It's not that I have a bias (although **yes,** I'd certainly prefer that they were healthy instead of sick). I typically don't have a preference whether we go to the doctor or not, I just want to do whatever is best for my child.

Naturally, I don't want to go to the doctor and pay $150 to hear that my kid is fine and just needs extra fluids and rest, but neither would I want the opposite: to forgo the doctor's visit only to discover later that something is very wrong and we should have gone (and now the doctor's office is closed and I'm facing an even costlier emergency room visit). In a case like this, I don't care either way, I just want to do what's best for my child, but I am much too close to the situation to get a straight answer.

In these situations, it is my fear of being wrong that prevents me from getting a reliable answer from Truth Testing. This is where third-party verification is a godsend. I usually call up my dear friend Alissa because she's a badass intuitive, but also because she's raised six children, so she's pretty much seen it all and has a crapload of natural remedies stored in her memory banks.

It's not just kids that can create a situation that's too close to home for you: you could run into this issue when it comes to two equally good job offers, the decision whether or not to move cross-country, elective surgery and operations, timing issues, high-stress situations, and whole lot more.

Typically, you will know when you're too close to the situation because you'll feel it. It's that sense of "OMG I just don't know what to do or think" and you can save yourself some time and some stress by calling in your Alissa to check in and see what's what.

What You Can Use in a Pinch

Sometimes you find yourself wanting to check in, but there's no pendulum in sight. Never fear! There are plenty of household objects that can be used in a pinch.
For example:

❖ cell phone dangling from charging cable

- ❖ keychain with keys

- ❖ luggage tag

- ❖ water bottle

- ❖ purse or strappy wallet

- ❖ tea bag

- ❖ washer on a string

- ❖ ring or pendant on a chain or necklace

- ❖ needle and thread

- ❖ bracelet

- ❖ fuzzy dice from your rearview mirror

- ❖ laptop charger

- ❖ a cherry dangling from its stem

- ❖ Get creative! What else can you come up with?

By the way, if you'd like your very own custom-made pendulum, just visit **http://custompendulums.com** and we'll hook you up, yo.

Earlier in this book, I promised to show you a technique that you can use for Truth Testing when you don't want to be conspicuous with a pendulum. I call it the Body Sway.

The Body Sway

This is a great way to use the principle of the pendulum with nothing more than your own body. It's also helpful when you wish to be discreet, like in a snooty store or in front of your mother-in-law, or the pharmacist. The body sway works basically the same as the pendulum, except you use your body as the pendulum.

Step 1: Calibrate.

Stand up straight with both feet planted firmly on the ground and your weight evenly distributed (in other words, don't lean to one side). Take a deep breath and let it out. While relaxed, ask for the first sign: *Please show me a clear sign for* **yes.** Relax and see what you notice. Your body will do something. Whatever you feel or notice in your body is your own personal sign for **yes.** Whenever you ask a question using Body Sway and you get that reaction, that's your **yes.**

Now return to that relaxed standing position and calibrate for the second statement: *Please show me a clear sign for* **no.** Notice your body's reaction. Does your body do something different? Again, take note of this as this will be your standard sign for **no.**

Return once again to that relaxed stance and ask for the final sign: *Please show me a clear sign for* **need more info.** What do you notice or what does your body do? This is your sign for **need more info.**

What if you get the same sign for more than one answer? No worries, just recalibrate and this time alter your question slightly: *Please show me a clear sign for* **yes,** followed by *Please show me a different sign for* **no,** and then *Please show me a different, third sign for* **need more info.**

Step 2: Phrase Your Question Mindfully

By now you should be a pro at asking a well-phrased question. Ask your Body Sway question the same way you'd ask a question with a pendulum, either out loud or in your mind. Be clear and specific, stick to just one variable, and avoid predictions.

Step 3: Relax and Await Movement

You've got your signs, you've asked your question, and now you just relax until your body begins to sway or lean. Once it does, you've got your answer. Easy, right?

Take a minute to try it now if you haven't already done so.

Here are the "standard" signs for the body sway. These are not absolute, and if you have different signs, don't sweat it. If you have unusual signs, you may find that over time, they normalize to these:

Yes = body sways forward

No = body sways backward

Need More Info = body remains still

Easy, right? The Body Sway is handy for a number of situations, and some people find they like it better than a pendulum. Know that sometimes, you may feel a **yes** or **no** in your body before your body begins to sway. I recommend you go with whatever works.

What if It Just Won't Move?

In most cases, if your pendulum won't budge, it's because the question is faulty. This is easily rectified by rephrasing the question, following the suggested guidelines in this book. If that doesn't work, it simply might not be optimal to know, or this might not be the optimal time to know. If you've rephrased the question and can't get movement, try asking again later. It is in your best interest to do this.

For example, once I was trying to book a flight, and I was using my pendulum to check optimal dates and times, as I always do. But when it came time to pull the trigger and actually book the flight, my pendulum wouldn't budge. I got frustrated and walked away. Later that day, I received new information about the dates, which meant the flight I was planning to take would have created a major conflict in my schedule. Because I listened to my pendulum, I saved a fortune in airline change fees. This is just one of countless stories of the magic of following guidance from the pendulum. Got your own stories? Share them with me on **Facebook;** I'd love to hear from you.

Other times, your pendulum may refuse to move if you have a bias. Or, there could be a weird reason, like the ones we discussed (too close to the situation, not optimal to know right now, etc.). It is also possible that you have a past-life trauma that's carrying over into this lifetime. If you were a witch who was burned at the stake, you might not be able to make a pendulum move because you're still carrying those old wounds of persecution. If that's the case, you will usually find that your pendulum moves once you clear the old past life trauma. For more information about how to perform energy clearings, get my book *1-2-3 Clarity! Banish Your Blocks, Doubts, Fears, and Limiting Beliefs Like a Spiritual Badass.*

CONCLUSION

Over time, you will most likely develop an affinity for your pendulum. Like me, you may wish to have more than one to keep on your person or around the house.

It is my sincerest hope that using a pendulum for Truth Testing will enrich your life, facilitate easier decision-making, empower you to make better choices for yourself, and overall, make your life easier and happier. And you're welcome to check me on that.

BLESSINGS.

THANK YOU

Thank for you taking the time to read *Pendulum Mojo*. I hope you've enjoyed learning about Truth Testing as much as I've enjoyed writing this book for you. If you implement what you've learned, you'll soon find that life gets easier and better every day.

By the way, if you enjoyed this book, please take a minute to write an honest review on Amazon or recommend the book via social media. Share your experiences and invite others to check it out. This will assist people just like you in discovering the many ways that Truth Testing can enhance their lives.

If you're willing, I'd love to have you come by my Facebook page and share your experiences with us. You never know who you might inspire and uplift with your story. **http://facebook.com/askamyanything**

WANT MORE PENDULUM MOJO?

Visit this site for videos, tips, and to learn about the "Ultimate Mojo" experience:

http://PendulumMojo.com

OTHER BOOKS
BY AMY SCOTT GRANT

1-2-3 Clarity! Banish Your Blocks, Doubts, Fears, and Limiting Beliefs Like a Spiritual Badass

2015 Boom: The Personal Almanac System That Will Change Your Year

Change Agents with Brian Tracy

WANT A UNIQUE PENDULUM OF YOUR OWN?

Would you like to have (or gift) a beautiful custom pendulum? These handmade creations are one of a kind, infused with vast quantities of love and healing energy. We work with your specific guides and energy team to select colors and gemstones especially for you.

Plus, when you make a purchase, you are supporting a young entrepreneur in fulfilling her goals and dreams. These pendulums make truly unique and memorable gifts for yourself or a loved one.

http://CustomPendulums.com

BEFORE YOU GO...
GET YOUR MOJO BACK!

Meet my son Adam. Adorbs, right?

I had an epiphany when he was two and a half years old and he started saying "dimmit." He struggled to open his water bottle... "dimmit!" He dropped a toy... "dimmit!" When he couldn't get his shoe on properly ("dimmit!"), that's when I finally figured out what he was saying.

And I thought, DAMMIT!

I had stopped paying attention to something I need to pay attention to—in this case, watching what I say around my little two-legged mimic.

Luckily, my oopsie was easy enough to fix. The next morning, I taught him to say "shoot!" and "rats!" and "bummer." I know, they're not nearly as colorful as the ones I prefer, but there's time enough for that later. He was still young, so he pronounced them as "shoot, ratsch, and bommer."

That's enough about Adam and me—**let's talk about YOU.**

- ❖ Are your oopsies easy enough to fix, or do some of them feel like colossal whoppers?

- ❖ Do you feel like you jacked up something important? Like a relationship. Or your career. Or your *life*.

❖ Think you missed out on a great opportunity?

❖ Does it seem like nothing is going your way, you're stuck, and it sucks?

❖ Or maybe you feel like you lost your mojo, and nothing is moving forward for you right now.

If any of that sounds familiar, then you deserve a private session with me. We call this the "Get Your Mojo Back, Dimmit" session.

By the end of this phone call, here's what you will have:

❖ Complete clarity around where you went off-track and how to fix it fast

❖ A faster, easier way to move you forward than you ever thought possible

❖ A blueprint of the next steps to powerfully move you forward and get you un-stuck

❖ A great sense of clarity and relief, as though the smoke has cleared and now you can see what to do

❖ Peace with the past and enthusiasm about what's next

And as a bonus, I'll help you identify the blocks that are still standing in your way, so you'll know what needs to be cleared to get what you really want.

My normal rate is $800 per session. The Mojo session is a special deal (translation: deeply discounted for you, dear Seeker).

Go here to get the scoop and book your Mojo session now:

http://spiritualasskicker.com/mojo.html

Are you ready to get un-stuck? Are you ready let go of the past and all the reasons you haven't yet?

Are you ready to **Get Your Mojo Back, Dimmit?**

Grab one of the available spots now before they're all gone. Otherwise, you'll be the one saying "dimmit."

ABOUT THE AUTHOR

Thanks to her highly developed intuition and insatiable quest for human advancement, Spiritual Ass Kicker **Amy Scott Grant** has healed and helped tens of thousands of individuals in more than thirty countries through her speaking, writing, and mentoring. Her extraordinary gifts are peppered with a unique sense of humor and a healthy dose of levity.

In September 2013, Amy was inducted into the National Academy of Bestselling Authors and received a prestigious Quilly award at the Golden Gala Awards in Hollywood, California. She was selected as a Thought Leader of the Year Finalist in 2013.

Amy has created a number of successful courses and digital products, including **Ripple Magic Leadership,** HIY (Heal It Yourself): Higher Power Tools, and MindTime™ meditations for kids at KidCentered.com. You can find Amy's writing all over the internet, as well as in the bestselling book *Inspired Marketing* by Dr. Joe Vitale and Craig Perrine; the acclaimed *Chicken Soup for the Soul: Life Lessons for Mastering the Law of Attraction*; the #2 bestseller *Change Agents* with Brian Tracy; and her *Spiritual Ass Kicker Series*.

Connect with Amy and discover what else is on the horizon at **www.AskAmyAnything.com**